I'm No Quitter!

by Dollie Fowler

To Sarah
Best Wishes
We Love You
Dollie Fowler
3/25/2024

I'm No Quitter
by Dollie Fowler

Copyright © 2015

Library of Congress Number: 2015951648
International Standard Book Number: 978-1-60126-467-1

Printed by
Masthof Press
219 Mill Road
Morgantown, PA 19543-9516

Chapters

Prologue 4
Acknowledgements 7
Childhood Years 8
A Happy Year 18
Teen Years 24
Young Married Life 30
Keith, A Special Angel 33
A New Baby and Town 50
The Play's the Thing 54
Dad, the Preachers' Son 59
Christina Lynn 65
Christina and Sabrina 70
Mark, He Mark Gave His All 71
Bill 95
Billy 102
Ernie, Actor and Priest 106
The Wreck 112
God's Plan 133
Third Time's Charm 136
Freedom Chapel Dinner Theatre 139
The Canadian Connection 146

Prologue

Many of my friends and relatives have been encouraging me to write this story. I have been through many tragic incidents in my life, and the last was on May 24, 1997. If I accomplish only one thing with my memoir, it would be to help others get through difficult times in their life. Every time I've had something terrible happen, I've asked why me? With each incident, it has made me a much stronger person. I am a survivor!

My childhood was difficult at times. Some of it was very happy, but there were times when it was anything but happy. I was an abused child along with my siblings. My sisters have given me their permission to write about our childhood, and the physical punishment we received from our mother. I'm sure this will shock many readers, and also the people who knew us when we were growing up. They had no idea what was taking place. Not even our father knew.

There is no greater grief for a mother than having a child die. I have lost two children. Mark, an Airborne Ranger in special forces and Keith, a little "angel" with leukemia. Also, two spouses have died, Bill at 47 with congestive heart failure and Ernie from a tragic car accident, that involved both of us. My dad and step mom lost their lives in a car wreck and my mom died in the bathtub. She just went to sleep and didn't wake up. All three of my siblings have passed on in recent years, my two sisters with cancer and my brother with kidney disease. I am now married to my third spouse, Lionel Caldwell.

Please don't feel sorry for me as you read this book. My life has had many twists and turns, and because of these events, one has to make many choices. The choices you make today will effect you for the rest of your life. If a few years ago, I had been told that I would own a dinner theatre and would be writing plays for the theatre, I would have told you, no way! You never know where your path in life will take you. This goes to show, you never know what you can do, until you have been put to the test. Just believe in yourself, and don't let anyone tell you that you can't do it!

I started writing my story about 12 years ago. Some of the chapters have been so difficult for me, bringing up memories from years gone by, and some in most recent years.

My goal in writing my memoirs or life story, is to let those who read this know that they can go on, and survive when tragic events happen in their lives. It's not easy, but you can do it! You'll become a stronger person, and remember, God never gives us more then we can handle. I'm not going to preach to you as I write this, and it is told in very simple words.

Before my sisters and brother passed on to a better place, they had encouraged me to finish this book. In writing this, there were times when I cried so much, I didn't think I would ever stop. This journey has been very emotional for me, but if I can help just one person to understand and accept the events that have taken place in their lives, then I feel my past years have been well spent. There are a few tears trickling down my cheeks now. I know I shouldn't feel upset with my tears, but I do. When strong sad emotions take over it's very hard to keep a happy face. People tell me that I'm strong, and they wonder where I get my courage and strength. Sometimes it's hard to always put on a happy face. Words can't explain all the hurt I have inside. Why have I had to cope with so much tragedy in my life? Maybe I'll never know.

Can you comprehend having surgery 7 times in 20 months? The tragic death of a spouse, a funeral while being a patient in the hospital, being handicapped and needing 24 hour care? Sometimes I wonder how in the world I got through all of this. The answer is faith, family, dear friends and a wonderful support group.

God spared my life for a reason, and I hope I can help others who are going through difficult times in their lives, by sharing my story. A friend wrote on a Christmas card, "You are certainly a profile in courage". I just did what I had to do, to survive.

I'M NO QUITTER!

Acknowledgements

This book is dedicated to my three siblings, Ruth Erlene, Billie Virginia Kay and Gerald Floyd Edds. They all left this world within two years of each other and I dearly miss them.

Dan Neidermeyer, a dear friend, who seemed more like a brother to me, who motivated and gave me the encouragement I needed to write my first Amish play. This turned into five Amish shows. He would challenge me and was always there whenever I needed him.

Lionel Caldwell, my husband, has been patient, listened to my stories and given me advice when needed.

Dianne Danz my dear friend, who has written several books and was so kind to edit my book.

Childhood Years

As you read about my young childhood years and what my Mother put we children through, people may think what a terrible person she must have been. What I now know, is that she was mentally ill. I will never forget what happened to me, but I do forgive her for all the pain and confusion she caused in my life.

I remember a few events that took place as far back as three or four years of age. My sister, Ruth Erlene, was nineteen months older and Billie Virginia Kay was two years and eight months younger than I was. Gerald Robert Floyd my brother, came along November of 1945, five years younger. We three sisters were born in Ohio, and my brother was born in Arkansas. My Dad was born and raised in Ohio and my Mom in Kansas.

My parents, Floyd and Ruth, were introduced to each other by my Mom's cousin, Pauline, who was dating my Dads brother, Paul. I don't know how long my parents dated before they were married, but I think it was less than a year. Dad was tall, handsome, with dark wavy hair and blue green eyes. Mom was petite, reddish brown hair, dark brown eyes and beautiful. They made a very attractive couple. It was after they were married that Mom found out Dad was younger then she, but they were in love, so it didn't matter. I think they were very happy for the first few years.

One of my earliest memories was when Dad left home for the Army during World War ll. I remember standing on a bench outside the train station in Lima, Ohio. I was four years old and searching the train windows, looking for his face to appear. When I saw his handsome smiling face looking out at me, I was filled with such joy and happiness. My little hand was waving as fast as it could wave, and Dad had a big smile on his tanned handsome face as he waved back at me. I think my sister, Erlene was standing along side me. I don't remember anything else about that day, but how sad I had become all of a sudden, missing my Dad, with tears running down my cheeks as the train disappeared from my view.

Maybe this is when my life as a happy child started to change. Mom was not happy with Dad, because he volunteered for the Army. He was not drafted like other young men, because he was married with three small children. He could have stayed home with his family, but that didn't matter to Dad, he just wanted to do what he could for his country and see the world or maybe just get away from home. After basic training Dad spent the last nine months of the War in France and Germany driving a supply truck in the front lines during many battles. He was in General Patton's Army.

Soon after Dad sailed to France, we moved to Springdale, Arkansas to live. We had family on my Mom's side living in the area, Grandparents, aunts, uncles, and cousins. From Ohio to Arkansas we traveled by bus and train. I remember we were crossing the Mississippi River on a high bridge and in the dining car eating, when the train started to shake a lot and I was scared and started to cry when Erlene said, "Watch out! The train is going to fall in the river." From that day on, I have been afraid of high bridges, crossing over water. I'll drive across them, but I always get a little nervous until I get to the other side.

We lived in Springdale and shared a home with my Mom's sister, and her four boys. It was a small house, but when you're only four years old, everything looks larger than it really is. Most of what I remember starts from this period. I was too young to understand most of what was going on around me. My sisters and I were never allowed to play and get dirty as most kids growing up. Our hair was always in curls and we wore dresses all the time, never allowed to wear long pants. If we didn't stay clean we'd be in trouble and get a spanking. All the pictures I have as we were growing up, always shows us in dresses.

I don't know when Mom and Dad started having problems with their marriage, but they got a divorce soon after Dad got out of the Army. My brother Jerry was born before Dad came home from overseas. I was so thrilled when my Grandma Edds, Dad's mother, came to visit us in Springdale. She wore her hair pulled back in a bun and had such a kind face. When Grandma opened her suitcase, she gave each of us a box of Dots candy. I had never had a box of candy all to myself until then. Boy, was that candy good!

Mom didn't like Grandma Edds, and was very upset with her visit. I think Grandma came for that visit because that's when my parents divorce took place. As far as I can remember this could be when the abuse started. Sometimes when a person is going through stressful times they take it out on others around them. I remember having bobby pins, before they had rubber tips on them, pushed into my scalp, when Mom would be putting up our hair in curls. It hurt a lot and if you cried it didn't matter, she would just keep on doing the same thing. If we didn't do as she wanted us to do, Mom would run her finger nails into our hands and this would cut our little hands and they would bleed. My sisters and I still have the scars on our hands and arms from many years ago.

Mom worked in a chicken factory when we lived in Springdale, and she didn't have a babysitter for my brother Jerry, after he was born. My sister Erlene, who was only seven years old, watched Jerry during the day, while Mom was at work. Erlene was taught how to change Jerry's diaper and give him his bottle. The door was to be locked from the time Mom went to work until she came home. My younger sister Billie and I went to a nursery school during the day, and I remember, that we were always given a tablespoon of cod liver oil every day, to keep us healthy. It tasted awful, almost as bad as castor oil, which is the worst tasting flavor of anything in the world.

During the 1940s, the world was a much safer place for people to live. One sunny Saturday afternoon, my sister Erlene and I wanted to go to the movie. We were five and seven years old. Mom gave us money for our movie tickets, and we walked the few blocks up town to the theater. We were shocked when we arrived and tried to buy our tickets, only to be told that there was no charge that day, it was free. We were thinking about all the candy and popcorn we could buy with the money we were going to have, since we didn't have to buy movie tickets. As we walked into the dark theatre, we didn't see any children and we thought that was strange. All we saw were adults, and we couldn't figure out why they were there to see a Roy Rogers movie. We sat in our seats discussing why there were no young children at the movies and we could hear people commenting on how cute we were to be setting in the theatre. So we just sat there waiting and waiting, as we saw speaker after speaker walk up on the stage and talk. The audience would cheer after each speaker and we had no idea what they were talking about. Finally, one kind woman asked us why we were at the theater and, of course, we told her that we had come to see the movie. She told us there was no movie, it was some kind of political rally being held in the theater. We were shocked! We didn't even know what a rally was, and we were very disappointed that there was no movie that day. After sitting there for about two hours eating popcorn and candy, we pulled our little bodies from our seats and walked back home. On the way home, I stepped off the curb and almost got hit by a car. Boy, did that scare me! My sister pulled me back and I held tightly to her hand all the way home. Isn't it strange the incidents in ones life that you will remember? Why would our mom send us to a theater when we were so young by ourselves? I don't know. If I tried to give you an answer I would be guessing, so I won't even try to answer that question.

When Dad came home from the Army, my parents remarried. It was June of 1946. Dad moved the family back to Ohio and I was a very happy six year old. I started the first grade and loved school. School was a very happy time for me, but, when I came home, the minute I stepped off the school bus I became very fearful of what would happen when I went into the house. If Mom had a bad day, I knew the rest of my day, along with that of my oldest sister, would be hell. I was always scared until my Dad came home from work. Mom did not abuse us when anyone else was near her. We were always threatened by her, that if we told anyone what she did to us, we would get it much worse than what we had just received from her. We were afraid to tell anyone, even our Dad.

One fall day after school, we three girls were playing outside and noticed smoke coming from the roof of the house. I told Mom about the smoke and she didn't believe me and told me to go outside and play until supper was ready. We sat on the running board of the car and watched the smoke. My sister and I sat watching the smoke and flames, discussing which one of us was going to go back inside the house to tell Mom again. When we saw more flames on the roof, we went back into the house to tell Mom for the second time. This time we got her attention! She ran outside and saw the flames and yelled upstairs to Dad. Dad was mixing his poultry feed and putting it into boxes. The farmers swore by that feed, they loved it. Their hens laid more eggs and were more healthy when they were fed Dad's feed.

We lived in the country and didn't have a phone, so Mom sent us to the neighbors to call the fire department. The flames could be seen from miles away. Men driving home from work, seeing the smoke and flames, arrived to help Dad carry furniture from the house. The fire started in the kitchen chimney. When the fire department arrived, the only water they had was what was on the tanker. I'm sure there is more to the story, but I don't remember it.

Our house burnt to the ground, while we children sat on the running board of the car watching it burn. This event in my life has left its mark on me. I hate fire to this day and feel like I've been branded by the flames. The next day we went back to look at the house, got out of the car, and walked through the charred rubble. On the stairs, I found a comic book that had not been burned. I couldn't believe it....the house burned down, but the comic book was not touched by the fire. How strange!

You're probably wondering what did Mom do to us, that was so bad. We would get spanked with anything she could get her hands on, hair brush, pancake turner, etc. One time I was told to go outside and get a green stick from a tree, I was six or seven at the time. Have you ever been spanked with a stick that you, picked from a tree? I had raised welts on my upper thighs and butt for days. No one could see them because my clothes covered all the marks. We were always threatened not to tell anyone or else we would get another spanking worse than the one we had just gotten. Erlene and I would say, "What did we do?" Mom would always say, "You know what you did!" She could be mad at someone or something, and her frustrations would be taken out on her children.

Why were we abused? I don't know. We were very well behaved children. Just ask anyone who knew us and they'd tell you what perfect children we were. We were scared to death not to behave. I could look at Mom the wrong way, and that would set her off. Sometimes we were told to put our tongues out and she would reach out and twist them. My cousin told me that story just a recently, she was there when it happened, I didn't remember that one. The skin of our arms would be pinched and twisted and as we got older we got our faces slapped a lot. I think I must have been fifteen or sixteen when Mom slapped me for the last time. As her arm came back to hit me, I reached out and caught her hand, and told her, "if you ever hit me again, I'll slap you right back." Mom had a shocked look on her face like she couldn't believe I had grabbed her hand, but she never hit me again.

When I was seven I needed a new pair of shoes, and Mom didn't have time to take me to the shoe store so she ask Dad to take me. I had always wanted a pair of black Patton leather shoes, but Mom wouldn't let me have them, because it wasn't a good shoe for school. That day I tried on brown tie shoes, that would be good for school, but when I saw the shiny black Patent leather shoes, I ask Dad if I could try them on and they fit so well. I told dad they felt better than the leather shoes, and he bought them for me. I was so happy with my first pair of black patent leather shoes. The clerk asked if I wanted them put in a box and I said no, I wanted to wear the shoes. I was smart enough to know if I wore them home and scuffed them up a little on the bottom, that Mom couldn't return them to the store. She almost had a heart attack when she saw my new black shoes. I had the biggest smile on my face and Dad did too. I was so elated. I loved those shoes!

When I was nine my parents were getting their second divorce from each other. Erlene and I wanted to live with Dad. Billie and Jerry were too young to say who they wanted to live with. The Judge asked for Erlene and me to be in the Courtroom for the hearing. He wanted to ask us who we wanted to live with. I was happy that my parents were getting a divorce.

The night before we were to appear in Court, Mom threatened us again, saying we had better say, we wanted to live with her, or else! We got a very hard spanking that night to remind us what it would be like if we didn't choose her over Dad. The Judge asked us if our Mom was abusing us in any way and we had to get up on that stand, with Mom looking at us, in the Courtroom and lie. That killed me and my sister. Just think, we were almost safe and now my heart was truly broken. I remember the look on Dad's face when we chose Mom over him. It broke my heart and I cried. I think the Judge knew what had happened. There was no divorce! Erlene and Dollie in picture.

A Happy Year

When I was in the sixth grade, I lived with my mother's youngest sister in Springdale, Arkansas. My grandmother was sick with breast cancer and Aunt Edith wanted me to live with her family for the next year. Mom thought it was because her sister needed help with Grandma, but I knew the truth. Aunt Edith wanted me to stay with her, because she had always wanted a daughter. Boy, was I a happy eleven year old. This was one of the best years of my life. My cousin Dennis and I would come home from school almost every day and ride his horse. I loved horses and was so happy. As a young girl, I aways said, "When I grow up, I'm going to marry Roy Rogers and live on a horse ranch."

Living with my uncle Bud, aunt Edith, cousin Dennis and my Grandma Dollie, was a wonderful treat for me. I couldn't believe that there was, no more hair pulling, spanking, pinching and slaps. It was like living in Paradise.

My parents and siblings, moved from Ohio to Denver that year. Mom had relatives living in Denver. She was born in Kansas near the Colorado boarder, so most of her family settled in Kansas and Colorado. Mom was finally home and I believe she was very content. Mom never liked Ohio. I don't know how my siblings felt about the move. Dad was such a friendly person, with a great sense of humor. He could live anywhere and fit in.

My Grandma Dollie died in the spring from breast cancer. It was a very sad time for me. I remember the night she passed away, my aunt made a bed for me on the couch in the living room, because Grandma and I shared a bedroom. I knew something was happening but pretended I was asleep. The doctor came and a little later more people arrived. Then I saw a cart being wheeled by me with a white sheet over someone, and I knew it was Grandma. I was named after her and people always asked me, what's your real name? I'd say, "Dollie, after my grandmother."

We had a funeral in Springdale and another one in Colby, Kansas, where Grandma was born and raised her family. I traveled on the train with my aunt Edith and Grandma's casket to Colby for the family funeral.

All Mom's sisters and brothers arrived with their children. The service was very large, with friends and family. It was like a huge reunion. My great great grandparents were some of the first to settle this area of Kansas. Later in the day my family went back to the cemetery to visit Grandma's grave. On our way, we were in a dust storm and it was awful. I never saw so much dust and tumble-weed. Dad had to stop the car, because he couldn't see to drive and the dust was inside the car. It was everywhere. Mom noticed that someone had moved the flowers she had put at the top of the grave and replaced them with other flowers. She was upset about this and was going to get to the bottom of who had switched the flowers.

Mom found out, that her brother's wife had moved her flowers from the head of the grave. What makes the difference as to whose flowers are at the head of the grave? I guess it did matter to Mom and my uncle's spouse, Ruth. Both women had the same name, Ruth. They confronted each other and found out who was responsible for the switch, and the name calling started in the front yard of my aunt's house. This was followed by hair pulling, hitting and rolling on the ground with each other. They were both dressed in beautiful suits and back in 1952, women wore garter belts with their hose. Their skirts were up around their waist. I couldn't believe my eyes. My dad and Uncle Bert had to separate their spouses. Mom's sister Rachel, ran into the house and came back with her camera to take pictures. The rolling on the ground by two adult women was a sight to behold. I thought it was one of the funnest things I had ever seen, but of course I was only 12 years old.

The next day all the families traveled back to their homes. I returned to Springdale with Aunt Edith and my family went back to Denver. It was during the train ride back to Springdale, I found out that I had to move to Denver with my family after school was over in May. I was disappointed and upset, because I didn't want to move to Denver. My wonderful world was about to fall apart.

School was over the middle of May and I was now twelve years old. Shortly after that, Aunt Edith and I were on a bus on our way to Denver. I was very sad and didn't want to go, but I didn't have any say in the matter. But I did miss my family and would be happy to see them again. I often wondered how they were coping with everyday life in the mile high city.

We had what seemed like a short summer, and before you knew it school was starting. I liked school. It was a very large school with many students and activities to choose from. I loved music and choose chorus and band. My family couldn't afford to buy me an instrument, so I had to play something that the school had in stock. I was given a bassoon, a double reed instrument to learn. What a wonderful instrument! I loved it. I was told it was a very difficult instrument to learn to play, but I thought it was easy.

Every morning, I couldn't wait until it was time to go to school and get out of the house. My parents were having problems again and when this happened Mom always took her unhappiness out on us kids. Dad had a good job, but things were not going well at home. My Dad drank when he was unhappy, although I never saw him drink liquor at home. He would do his drinking in bars.

I'm No Quitter!

One day in early summer, Dad told us that he was going back to Ohio. They couldn't live together any longer. Erlene and I weren't surprised. We were older and could understand what was happening and very sad over Dad's leaving.

Erlene had been writing to Dad and told him that we wanted him to come back to Denver to get us. When Erlene told me Dad was coming, I couldn't believe it. I was so excited. I didn't know how this would even be possible, since Mom would never allow us to leave with him.

We were told not to tell Mom that Dad was on his way to Denver. He arrived with his sister and her husband Judy and Ed Fry. We considered Ohio to be our home. Dad first picked up Erlene and me, at our grandfathers house, my mom's dad. We then drove to our house to get my clothes. Mom was home from work when we arrived and said she wouldn't give me any of my clothes. My dad found a police officer and told him the story. The officer went with us to the house, so I could get my clothes.

You're probably thinking, how could that even be possible, a father taking a child from the mother and crossing state lines? Well, the laws were different in 1953, and it was legal. I can't tell you how happy I was, but also sad, because we were leaving my younger brother and sister behind.

My aunt Judy Fry told me that I sang, "Your Cheating Heart," all the way home. This song was very popular at the time. Hank Williams, the country singer made this song a classic.

I'm No Quitter!

The year I lived in Springdale Ark. I saw Hank Williams sing this song at a local school. Over 50 years have passed and she is still telling that story, but I don't mind.

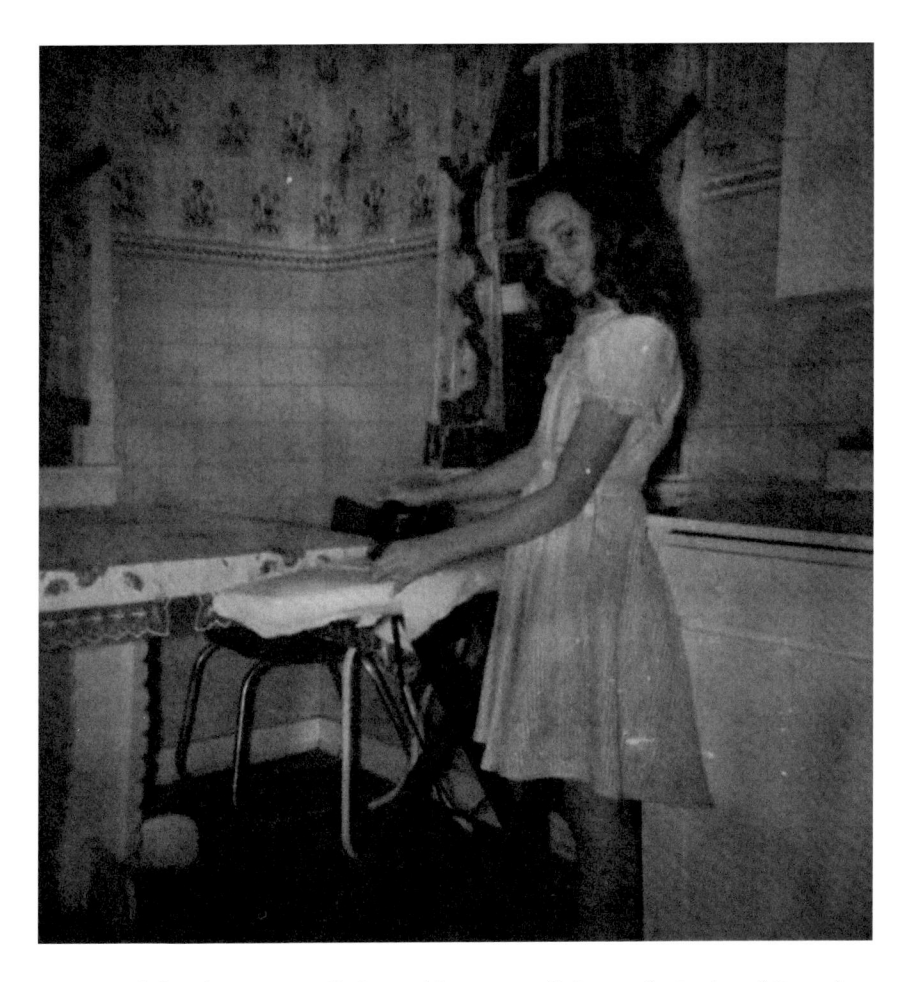

Springdale Ak. one year living with Aunt Edith, Uncle Bud and Dennis.

Teen Years

Erlene and I started school in Ohio and were very happy. We were again surrounded by a very large family. Dad let me stay with his sister Ethel during the week and go to school in Delphos. This was about 10 miles from where Dad and Erlene lived. The school in the small town where we lived only had four or five students in my class and I was used to going to a large school. I also wanted to play in the band so I needed a larger school. My cousin, John was a year older than I and we had such a good time that year. He was like an older brother to me. I was happy but I still worried about my brother and sister who were in Denver.

Dad had a surprise for Erlene and me after Christmas. He drove to Denver to get Billie and Jerry. He went to the school and picked them up without my Mom's knowing. She found out about it when the teacher called her at work and told her, they were missing from the school yard. I felt so bad and sad for Mom when I found out what happened. It was a drastic thing for my dad to do, but he wanted his children, so he just kidnapped them. Dad called Mom later in the day to tell her that he had Billie and Jerry. Today the laws have changed, and a parent would be in jail if they tried anything like this.

My parents started to speak on the phone and one thing led to another. Before you knew it, Mom was on her way to Ohio to reunite with Dad. What a bummer! I didn't like it at all. Don't get me wrong, I didn't wish my mom any ill will, I just thought it was wrong for my parents to continue living together. Isn't it amazing how people can put each other through so much hell and still love each other? Mom was back to stay.

My sister Erlene, got married right before she turned sixteen. Erlene was very mature for her age, and I thought it was a good move for her. She had a very loving husband and married into a wonderful family. I was happy for her, but I now felt very alone, thinking what's ahead for me!

I started high school in Oakwood, Ohio, I was fourteen. The whole family was back together again, Mom, Dad, Billie, Jerry and me. This time I was hoping everything would work out. If it wasn't for the erratic abuse, Mom would have been a good mother. She made a lot of our clothes, dresses, coats and we were always getting compliments on our beautiful clothes and she was also a great cook. There was nothing like her fresh fried bread.

We had to clean house before we went to school in the mornings, so I always made sure I got my homework finished at night. When I think about all the work we had to do during a day, I wonder how the children today would handle it, with their games, cell phones, personal computers and all the other gadgets they have.

I really loved school. Learning to play the oboe in band, another double reed instrument, was exciting and I was having so much fun. I loved music and singing. Making new friends was easy for me and. since I had attended a large school in Denver before coming to Oakwood, I seemed to be very popular with the students. I was having a wonderful time. Classes were very small, only about 30 in each class. This was a small country school with many of the students living on farms. It was a good mixture. A few years after I left Oakwood, the school district consolidated with Paulding County. Many schools did this in the early 1960s. They would close the small school and bus students to a larger school.

My years at Oakwood were filled with activities and fun times, and I have no regrets, life was good!

I'll never forget the night our pep band played at the basket ball game and we decided to drive to a near by town after the game for a hamburger. It was cold outside with snow and we had car trouble. There were five of us in the car and all in the band. We had to wake a farmer to help us with the car, it was stuck in the mud and our radiator had a crack in it. It was very late when I finally got home, after 1am. We had no cell phones back then and no way to get in touch with family, to let them know what had happened. My dad thought something awful had happened to me, and he had been to all the near by towns looking for me. The driver of our car came into the house to tell Dad what had happened, but Dad was so upset, he wouldn't even listen to what my friend had to say. I was so embarrassed. Dad was so mad at me, he wouldn't speak to me for a few days. I know he believed I was telling the truth, it's just that he didn't know where I was. A parent will stress out if they don't know where their children are. This is a fact.

It was exhilarating growing up with my siblings. Holidays were especially wonderful with all the relatives at my Grandparents house. A great time was had by all, with good food, conversation and games. These were some of the happiest memories of my life. Family is so special to me.

There are so many stories I could share with you, but this book would end up being thousands of pages. So, we'll leave well enough alone.

I met Bill Fowler when I was sixteen years old. He lived in Van Wert, Ohio and worked in a local drug store. The Oakwood band was marching in a big Peony parade in Van Wert. That day, it was so hot outside, about 90 degrees, and everyone was trying to escape from the heat. We were buying squirt guns and spraying each other with water to stay cool. I thought Bill squirted me with water while he was working in the drug store, and that's how our relationship started. By the way, he didn't squirt me, it was someone else.

We dated for quite sometime and going to two proms the same year was so much fun. I didn't plan to marry until I had finished college, but my plans didn't work out like I wanted them too. My dream was to someday become an actor and singer. Little did I know that this would happen later in my life.

As I grew up, I sang whenever I had the chance, church, chorus, talent contest, at home, in the car. One day I was invited to audition for the Lloyd Thaxton show in Toledo, Ohio, he was the Dick Clark of the Midwest. I was sixteen and the audition ended in a disaster. They put me in a big room that was all glass with a piano and microphone, I was scared to death. The TV crew was looking down at me, from a booth up above and said, "Whenever you're ready you can start." The piano accompaniment started, I sang the first verse and then forgot the lyrics to the song,but at least I didn't stop singing, I made the lyrics up as I continued singing. I couldn't believe what I had done, but at least I didn't quit singing. I wasn't surprised when they didn't call me back for the show. My home life wasn't going well, so when Bill ask me to marry him I said yes. I desperately wanted to go to college, but it would have to wait. I couldn't bear to live at home any longer. Acting and singing would have to wait. I was still a teenager, but my school days were now over.

Erlene 16 and 72

Young Married Life

We had a very small wedding with just family members attending. Bill's mother was so sweet and kind. His dad was sort of angry looking and I felt that he didn't care for me, but I was wrong. I later found out that he never wanted his son to get married until after he finished college. You don't always get what you want in life. I now had two new brothers and a little sister. We moved into a cute one bedroom apartment in Van Wert, and we were happy.

Cherries were in season and I thought I'd make my first homemade pie. I picked the cherries and pitted them by hand, made the piecrust and baked my pie. When it was time to eat the beautiful pie, I tried to cut it and the knife wouldn't cut through the piecrust. After phoning my mother-in-law, I knew what I had done wrong. I made the crust using only milk and flour, there was no shorting in the crust. The pie was has hard as a brick and I had to throw the it away. It was along time before I attempted another pie.

Bill worked for the New Central Railroad, and was skilled at his job. He started going to college part time, and we were expecting a baby in March.

Christina Lynn, was born March 9, weighing in at 5 pounds. What a beautiful little girl, with dark curly hair. She was so tiny she looked like a china doll. I was in the hospital five days and was determined to fit into one of my dresses when I came home from the hospital. I had gained 30 pounds and all my friends told me that I'd never be able to fit into a dress I wore before I became pregnant, but I did. I couldn't zip it up in the back, but I it work for me. By wearing a sweater over the dress, this way you couldn't tell the dress was open in the back. I just loved everything about being a mother. Then about 16 months later Mark joined our little family. This was the perfect family, a girl and a boy.

The same year we had a flood. The ground was frozen and it rained like crazy. With an increase in higher temperatures, there wasn't anywhere for the water to go, and if you lived near the creek you were going to be flooded. Our new car was totaled, the water reached the top of the car. The night of the flood, a girlfriend and I went to a movie and when I got home I parked the car along the side of the house. Since it was new, we didn't park the car on the street for fear it would get hit. A lot of good that did! We had so much water a motor boat came up to the porch to rescue us. A few months later, Bill was mowing the lawn, and turned his foot into the lawn mower, and it cut his toes off. The doctors were able to save his big toe, which helps a person keep their balance when they walk. I'll never forget the horrible sound it made. It was a grinding sound, like something was being chewed. He was in a cast for a few months after surgery, and had some broken bones, but in time everything healed.

A few months later Bill was laid off from the railroad and looking for a job. He was sent to Warsaw, Indiana for a job interview and was hired by R.R. Donnelly & Sons. This was a wonderful opportunity for our family. A new plant was being built and Bill began his apprenticeship as a photoengraver.

We moved to Warsaw and had another child. I was only 22 years old and now have three children. There isn't a lot of time for yourself when you have three pre-school children at home. I've always been very mature for my age and now it looked like I'd have my work cut out for me. There's nothing I loved more than being a mother.

Keith, A Special Angel

From the time Keith was born I knew he was a special child. How did I know that? Well, it's just something that a Mother knows. I'm sure some parents know what I'm talking about. He had a very short life but he left his mark on those he meant during his six years. There was a very bad blizzard the day he came into the world on December 19,1961 in the Warsaw Community Hospital in Indiana. I think we had received about two feet of snow on that cold snowy day. I had been rushed to the hospital when my contractions were about three minutes apart. The doctor came in to check on my progress and thought he had time to have office hours, thinking the baby was hours from being delivered. Boy was he wrong! A few hours later the babies head was crowning and the nurses couldn't wait any longer for the doctor and they rushed me into the delivery room. The doctor had been called, but because of the snow storm, he had a difficult time getting to the hospital. When the doctor finally arrived, Keith had already been born. Back in the 60's, they gave you ether to put you to sleep and the nurses were hoping this would stop my labor contractions, but it didn't. As I was regaining consciousness, I looked up and saw the Doctor standing over me with a big fur hat on his head, the kind that has the ears tied on top of the hat, and he was asking the nurse, "What did she have a boy or a girl?" When later I would ask him, if he made it to the hospital before the baby came, he lied to me and said, yes.

What a beautiful baby, with light red hair and dark brown eyes. After a five day stay in the hospital, Bill and I brought our new bundle of joy home on Christmas Eve. Chris and Mark thought he was the best Christmas gift they could ever have. I was so happy, life was good.

Once in a while if we could find a baby sitter, we would go out to a nearby restaurant and nightclub. When people found out I could sing, I was ask to preform with the featured group, so with a little coaching I gave in. That turned into a regular singing gig every time I showed up. I was having a great time!

I was a stay at home mother until I took a job with the Playhouse Company, they sold toys and gift items on the party plan in homes. I loved my job very much and it got me out of the house, a chance to meet other young mothers, and helped them shop for Christmas gift items in the comfort of their own homes. Bill was home with the children in the evenings so I didn't have to hire a baby sitter. I was making some extra money for Christmas and having fun at the same time. I could also earn books of "green stamps" depending on how high my sales were. The end of the season arrived and I had over 250 books of green stamp. When I redeemed them, it was like Christmas, what fun!

I did very well my first year and the Company ask me to take over as supervisor for them in Indiana and Ohio. I was responsible for the training and records for the women working under me in both states.

This was a job I really enjoyed and I got paid for it. I was having such a good time. What more could you ask for in a job? Before I could take on such a great responsibility, I had to take the company training in Minnesota.

This was a bad time for my family because Keith had been sick. He had a fever, his legs hurt at night and he would wake up crying because he hurt so bad. I'd sit on his bed at night and rub his legs until he would fall back to sleep. I took Keith to the doctor and he gave him medicine, but he only got worse. A few days later I took him back to the doctor, but it didn't do any good. He said Keith's illness would have to run its course and was a virus. Everyday it seemed that Keith got a little more weak and still running a fever. My baby was so sick!

I knew my son was very ill, but what does a mother do when the doctor says he'll be fine? The next day he got a terrible nose bleed and it wouldn't stop. The blood was rushing from his nose like a water facet. I called the doctor and he said to apply pressure on his nose and some ice. His little nose bled for quite some time. Keith was still running a high fever, so I took him to the hospital and told the doctor on call how ill he had been. A blood sample was taken from Keith and we were told that It would be a few days before the test results would be back. The hospital would let us know if there was a problem.

I was due to fly to Minnesota for a week of school and training for the Playhouse Company, but I felt like I couldn't go with Keith being so sick. I still didn't have the results of the blood test from the hospital. I had a very strong feeling that something was seriously wrong with my son. My good friend Barbara, who worked for a doctor, told me to go on the business trip and she would stop in every day and check on Keith. Bill said he would phone me if he thought I needed to come home early. So reluctantly, I flew off to St. Paul. I couldn't stop thinking about Keith.

Six days later Bill and the kids picked me up at the airport in Chicago. I took one look at my beautiful baby boy and I knew something was very wrong. Keith was pale and burning up with a high fever. He laid his little head on my lap and slept all the way home, as my hands stroked his beautiful red hair. It was late evening when we arrived home and I told Bill to drive directly to the hospital, I wasn't going to wait any longer for those test results. As a mother, I knew that I had to take charge and I couldn't wait another day to find out what was wrong with my son.

We sat in the emergency room of the hospital waiting to see the doctor who was, "On call". I explained about the blood test that was taken the week before, and I wanted to know what the results were. When I told the doctor why I had come to the hospital with my son, he just looked at me like, why are you bothering me on a Sunday for a little cold or flu! I wasn't going to leave the hospital until I had the results of those test. The doctor had to locate the key to unlock the lab and find the results of Keith's test.

Bill, Keith and I were sitting on chairs in the hallway as the doctor walked towards us. He knelt down beside Keith and when he did this, I knew it was going to be bad. The doctor said, " How would you like to stay with us for a while?" KEITH shook his little head no, and hung on to me with his little hands and wouldn't let go. I told him it was all right and I would stay with him and not to be afraid. I was scared to death!

To this very day, I can't understand how a hospital can do blood work on a person, and know that the results are very bad, and not contact the person or family. It doesn't make sense to me. This happened in 1967. I pray that nothing like this could ever happen again in our country today. A family should not be left in the dark!

The next day a doctor from a laboratory, near Chicago, came to the hospital to do a bone marrow test on Keith. We had to wait two dreadful days for the test results. Bill and I had been taking turns sleeping at the hospital at night and Keith seemed to be in good sprits for as sick as he was. When the test results finally arrived, I had a feeling I knew what they would show, but I didn't want to believe it. So, in a way I was not surprised when the doctor told me that Keith had leukemia. I had seen a show on TV about this type of cancer and I was shocked. What parent thinks their child is going to come down with such a terrible illness? I cried a lot, but not where the children could see me, and Bill kept telling me everything would be fine. Of course, I wanted to believe that everything would be all right, but deep down in my heart I knew that nothing would never be the same again. A person is never prepared when a tragedy strikes.

School started in September and all three children were in school. Keith was in kindergarten and loved school. People were drawn to him like a magnet and he loved everyone. One morning I was hanging clothes on the line in the back yard, when Keith came outside, looking up at the sky, on a beautiful sunny day, and said, " Mommy, how high up in the sky is heaven?" I answered his question as best as I could, and thought he was satisfied with my answer. He then went off to play, at least that's what I thought, but instead, he was getting the ladder out of the garage. When I ask what he was doing with the ladder, he said, " I'm going to climb up to heaven." He wanted to see heaven! Keith proved to me many times in his short life that he really was an angel.

It really hurts when your child comes home from school crying. Children can be very cruel to other children. Keith had a very full face from the drugs he was taking and the kids would call him, fat cheeks. Of course he couldn't help that his cheeks were fat, but try explaining that to a small child. We as parents do what we can to make our children happy.

A few months had gone by since Keith was diagnosed with leukemia. I later found out, that Keith was so sick when he was first admitted to the hospital, that they didn't expect him to survive. This, seemed to give me hope for his future. If anyone could beat this, it would be my little angel.

Keith was now in remission and our lives seemed to be getting back to normal, when Bill was offered a new job in New York. He wasn't going to accept the job, because he thought Keith wouldn't have any insurance if we moved. The new position was just what my husband needed and an opportunity like this doesn't come along but once in a lifetime. I told him to take the job and we would survive somehow. So Bill started the new position in the fall and I planned to move with the children after the first semester of the school year in January.

We settled in a new home in Farmingdale, Long Island, and all three children started school in their new school. Our family was doing well at this time and Bill's office was only five minutes from the house. We even moved our cat with the four kittens to NY. The kittens were only a few days old and the kids and I were not going to leave them behind, after all they were part of our family.

A few days later the children started their new school in Farmingdale. Keith was in kindergarten, Mark second and

Christina, in the third grade. Keith was still in remission and doing well. My first priority after the move was to find Keith a good hematologist. I was given the name of a well known doctor. He was on staff at Long Island Jewish Hospital. When I first met Dr. Levey, I felt he was the answer to my prayers. Keith took an instant liking to the doctor and I trusted Dr. Levey with my son. I had been told that he was the best hematologist in the country.

When we would go for office visits there would always be many children in the waiting room. I sat there looking at the other children and wondered what had brought them to Dr. Levey's office and wondering if they had the same illness as Keith.

When Keith started school along with Chris and Mark, he was in remission. He loved school and was so happy, but just when we thought everything was fine, we had the rug pulled out from under us. The next trip to the doctor wasn't good.

Keith was no longer in remission. I couldn't understand how this could happen. He was well one day and the next day he was sick again. When you have leukemia there's always that one wild, white blood cell, that is still hiding in your body and if you don't destroy them all, that one cell will totally take over the red cells. That's what happened to Keith. He would continue to go back and forth in and out of remission.

Keith loved attending church and for his six young years, he had a very deep Christian faith. I taught him to say his prayers before he would go to bed at night and they developed into such beautiful prayers. His prayers were so sincere and always about helping others. There was so much love in his soul for everyone, it didn't matter who it was.

Many times when a child is ill and he can't function with everyday activities, his brain will develop at a faster rate. It's the body's way of compensating for the illness. Keith loved to put 1000 piece puzzles together and didn't like it if anyone tried to help him. He would do it himself! His mind was so sharply developed for his six years. Most of his day was spent resting and sleeping. Bad bruises started to appear overnight on his skin. It looked like someone had beat him. This was blood under his skin, internal bleeding. It broke my heart to see my son like this. He looked so sad and was getting more weak with each passing day. As a mother, I wanted to do everything in my power to keep my child well. I would have gladly traded places with him. What mother wouldn't?

My little angel had to make a trip to the hospital for a transfusion and the experience was so painful for him. The doctors wanted a medical student to take the bone marrow from Keith and the student had an awful time putting the needle in his back to extract bone morrow. Keith was screaming and I tried to stop them, but the staff went ahead. Finally, I yelled for them to STOP! Don't touch him again! Get a doctor to do this now! This was so painful for him and I vowed that I would never let this happen to him again.

The next day as we were driving home from the hospital, Keith ask me, "Mommy, do I ever have to go to the hospital again?" My answer was, NO!

Keith wanted to go the Van Wert fair, the first week in September. He loved that fair so much. The doctor said he could go, but only for a few days, and to come to his office the day he returned home from the fair. We knew this would be one of Keith's last wishes. The next day Keith and Bill flew to Ohio for the fair and he had a great time! He was so happy when he arrived home and couldn't wait to tell me about his time at the fair. We drove to the doctors office after I picked them up from the airport and waited to see Dr. Levey. After the office visit and test, we were told to come back in 45 minutes. When we returned from our little drive, I went into the office alone. I knew what the news was going to be. I was wearing my sunglasses, because I didn't want the doctor to see me cry when he told me the news. After I was given the bad news, I asked about other treatments. He said none of them had worked and most of the children that I had seen sitting in his waiting room over the past six months had died. There seemed to be many seconds of silence in the room. It must be so difficult for a doctor to tell parents that their child is going to die. I know it takes special people to dedicate their lives to children and try to save their lives.

We were told Keith only had a few more days left to spend with his family. I knew this day was coming, but I was still in shock. We drove home in silence. Keith lay down for a nap and Bill went to work. Chris and Mark were in school. I sat in a quiet room, contemplating what I was going to do next. I went to the phone and called the doctor to ask if we could take Keith back to Ohio for his finial days, so he could see our family again. We had planned to travel home for the funeral. Dr. Levey said yes, but we had to leave by the end of the next day. We were on a plane out of JFK the next morning.

We were in the plane, flying high in the sky, with clouds around us that looked like marshmallows, and Keith took this time to talk about Heaven. When our meal was brought to us, I offered to cut his meat, but he said he'd do it himself. "What do you think I am, a baby?" He was so independent.

My dad picked us up at the airport and we stayed with Bill's parents in Van Wert. Family and friends stopped in to visit with Keith. He was very happy with his family, and it was wonderful seeing him laughing and enjoying his life.

The next day Keith wanted to lie on the couch during the day. He was so tired that I wanted him to lie down in a bedroom up stairs, but he wanted to be around people. It was about 3 o'clock when he said he wanted to take a nap, so Bill carried him upstairs. He asked me to lie down with him and as we were lying there in a dark room with my arm around him, his little voice said, "Mommy when I grow up, I'm never going to do anything to hurt anyone, I'm going to be just like that man Kennedy who was shot." It was all I could do to keep from crying like a baby. I reached over and stroked his beautiful red hair, and he said, "Mommy I'm going to go to sleep now and sleep like an angel."

Those were the last works my little angel spoke to me. The next day Bill carried him down to the couch, where he wanted to be. I sat holding his head on my lap until he drew his last breath. He was now in heaven where he wanted to be. I was happy for him. He was free of pain now.

Bill had made all the funeral arrangements, but I don't remember much about anything that was going on around me, except there were so many people. It was a big blur to me. I don't know who I spoke to or what I did for the next few days. I wondered what little Chris and Mark, must have been thinking. They loved their brother and had asked me if he was going to die. I tried my best to explain it to them so they would understand. They were very special children during this time. Just imagine how hard it is for a parent to adjust to all that is happening around them, but it must be so much more difficult for young children. It's difficult to know what children are thinking, they put on a good front.

My sister Billie and I went uptown to buy Keith a suit to be buried in. Back in the 1960's, you would have dressed your child in something dressy. I'll never forget the clerk in the shop, when I asked to see dress suits for a six year old. She said, " Is it for a wedding or special occasion?" I said, "it's for my son's funeral." Her mouth dropped open and she said she was sorry, she didn't know. Of course she didn't know! I told her it was all right and consoled her as she cried. I felt so bad for her. I bought Keith a little brown suit and he looked so beautiful in it with light auburn hair and a few freckles on his cheeks. Just like the little angel he was.

There must have been over 300 people at the funeral. Some came from as far away as New York State. I think I got through the service without crying, but I don't know how I did it. I know that I prayed to God a lot, to please give me the strength I needed to get through the day. It seemed like Chris and Mark didn't take their eyes off me all day. I knew I had to be strong for them.

Grandma Edds came to the funeral, but Grandpa Edds didn't attend. Grandma told me Grandpa just couldn't attend. He was having a hard time accepting why a child could die at such a young age ,when he was an old man and had many health problems. Grandpa felt he should have been the one passing on, not Keith.

Grandpa Jake Edds was a lay preacher, who was self taught, and whenever I would attend church with my grandparents growing up, I always felt entertained by the service. Grandpa was an excellent preacher. I loved going to church with them. Grandpa had a very deep faith in God, but Keith was the first young child in our family to die, and Grandpa took this very hard! As a person goes though life, there are many times when you ask…..why did this happen to me?

Late afternoon we were all back at Grandma Biddy's house and my mom asked me to come home with her for a few days. I didn't want to, but she was my mother and I thought maybe she needed me. Bill insisted that I take the children and spend the night with Mom and Dad. So I did. I was thinking of my parents at this time and how sad they must have been feeling. Bill said he would come for us the next morning.

We put some of the beautiful flowers from the funeral in the car so Mom could enjoy them. We had been at Mom and Dad's for a few hours when everything blew up. Dad, Chris and Mark were watching TV when Mom started on me about the flowers and wanting to know why I gave other people nicer flowers than I gave her. That statement put me in shock! I couldn't believe my ears! What was she saying? She went on and on, about how I gave others, flowers that were nicer than I gave her. I was horrified that she would say something like that, when her grandson had just been buried. Finally I broke down and cried. She wanted to know why I was crying and I said, "My son has just been buried, and the only thing you can think about, is that I gave someone else nicer flowers than I gave you." My dad came into the kitchen and wanted to know what was wrong, so I told him. By this time I was a walking zombie and didn't know what to do. I went to the bedroom and stayed there until the next morning.

Mom said she was sorry the next morning, but she should have been thinking about the grandson she had just lost, not flowers. It's so hard to understand why some people think the way they do and what motivates them to say what they say.

Keith had wanted a baby brother in the worst way. So many times he would ask me if I would get him a baby brother. Bill and I wanted another child, and I was hoping we would have another child while Keith was still with us. When I told Keith we were going to have a new baby, he was so happy, smiling and told everyone. When his dad came home from work that day he couldn't wait to tell his dad. I let Keith think he was the first one to know so he could break the news to the rest of the family. Keith died in September and Billy was born in March.

Keith had always wanted a horse, so we had a picture of a horse carved on the stone that marked his grave. Now he has his pony. My little angel is now happy and pain free living with Jesus in heaven.

A few days passed and we flew back to Farmingdale. I don't think anyone said much to each other on the plane. We all had different thoughts going though our heads, even the children. Chris and Mark were great, a little quiet and they didn't ask many questions. Sometimes we don't give children enough credit, but they know what's going on around them.

The kids started back to school, Bill went back to work, and I was alone with my thoughts. I missed Keith so much. What a rare young boy he was. You may have heard it said, *that the good die young.* All I know is, he was certainly good! It took me a few months to go though Keith's belongings. I just couldn't do it right away after returning home. Most of his toys and clothes were donated to the church. It was time for me to pick up the pieces of my life and go on. After all I had a family to care for and they needed me. I needed them too, so very much.

Keith's last Christmas.

Mark, Chris, and Keith.

Dad, Mom, and Keith (age 5)

A New Baby and Town

We are now moving to Schaumburg, near Chicago, and our baby is due in a few weeks. It would be difficult to move to a new town with a baby due soon, so the children and I would stay in Van Wert with Bill's family and wait for the baby to arrive. In the meantime, Bill found us a new home.

Bill drove 150 miles back and forth to Van Wert every weekend. Those few weeks seemed so long. I did a lot of walking, hoping it would bring on my labor, wanting to have this baby now! I had passed my due date and the doctor said he would induce my labor in a few days, if needed Finally, I was in labor and it was going fast. Bill had just gone back to Schaumburg and had to turn around and drive back to Van Wert. Early morning little William Eugene Fowler II was born. He was a perfect baby and in a fews days we would be on our way to our new home.

I was thinking a lot about Keith and feeling sad that he wasn't here for the birth of his new brother, but knew he was looking down from heaven with a happy smile on his face. I could picture his beautiful face, with the light auburn hair and freckles. Oh how I missed my precious Keith!

The new house was wonderful! We settled in and I made new friends and even learned to play bridge. The children started another new school. They had already gone to three schools in their young lives. When it snowed they had to walk to school and there was so much snow that winter. The rule was: you had to live one full mile from school before you could ride on the school bus. We were just under the one mile to the school.

A year later, we were moving to another new home. Bill had been offered a job in Lancaster, PA. and we decided it would be a good career move for him. We knew how beautiful the country was, because we had spent time there on a vacation a few years earlier. He started his new job in January, and in the spare time he was looking for a house, but wasn't having much luck. When spring arrived, it was time for me to made a trip to Lancaster to find a place for us to live.

We found a beautiful brand new townhouse in Akron. It wasn't quite finished, but by the time the family was ready to move, it would be completed. We moved to Lancaster County the end of May 1970. Billy had just turned a year old on March 25, Easter Sunday, and I'll never forget that day. Bill had flown home from Lancaster for the Easter weekend, and we had the worse blizzard the country had had in years. Several feet of snow fell over the weekend and many airports were closed. I'll never forget that storm, on Billy's birthday.

The airports reopened late Monday or Tuesday and Bill was able to fly back to Harrisburg. When he arrived, he couldn't find his car in the parking lot. It was covered up with snow, so he had to do some shoveling and digging to find it. That was a very memorable Easter weekend.

The next few months passed quickly and I was looking forward to moving to Lancaster County Pennsylvania. I had a very good feeling about this move. The country was beautiful, the people were down home and friendly, Bill loved his job and my children were happy and excited to move to a new area. They were fascinated with the horse and buggies of the plain people.

Moving has always been an adventure to me. It was exciting to meet new people and see different parts of America. Lancaster County was such a wonderful place to raise my children. Of all the places I've lived in my lifetime, Lancaster is my favorite. I always told my children to go out of their way and make a new child in their school feel welcome, remembering what it was like to be a student in a new school. I told them,"Introduce yourselves and to be their friend, help them get settled in their new surroundings." To my knowledge they always did this. I was very proud of them.

We all settled into our new home and were very contented and happy. Bill had a wonderful job, and I was happy staying home and being a mother. The kids were making new friends, and school would be starting in September. There was a void in my life, missing Keith, but I had one year old baby Billy to keep me busy.

Baby Billy

The Play's the Thing

My acting career started when Bill wanted me to audition for the musical, Gays and Dolls, and I was cast in the role of Adelaide. The American Business Association in Lititz produced the play as a fund raiser. There were so many songs and dance numbers in the show, and it was hard work, but I loved every moment of it. The play was just what I needed to take my mind off of the loss of Keith. Opening night, the audience numbered over 1000 people. Before I went out on stage, I could hear my heart beating, like it was coming out of my chest. I was a wreck! Usually, I wore contact lenses, but I chose not to wear them, because I didn't want to look out over the audience and see someone I knew, for fear of forgetting my lines.

A few years later, I was one of the charter members who was instrumental in saving the Ephrata Playhouse. The Ephrata Borough was considering tearing the building down. A small group of local citizens formed a committee to save the playhouse from being destroyed. The theatre had been a summer professional theatre called The Legion Star Playhouse. The producer from New York City, was John

Cameron, and he brought in well known actors such as Roy Scheider, Betty White and Ann B. Davis, to perform in summer stock.

A couple of the actors who auditioned and was turned down by the director from New York were, Robert De Niro and Sylvester Stallone. When we went through old files in the office of the theatre, we found their applications. Today both of them are famous actors. I learned something from this. Never let someone tell you you can't do something. If you have a dream....go for it! John Cameron produced shows in Ephrata from 1953 until 1972.

Our volunteer group began to present and produce plays in order to preserve the tradition of the theatre, "The Playhouse In the Park." Later it became known as .the Ephrata Performing Arts Center. The group grew and incorporated as a not-for -profit organization in 1979. The first season as EPAC was 1980.

I spent years on the board of directors and watched this wonderful theatre grow into a beautiful community theatre. Local actors performed in some of the finest musicals and dramas on the EPAC stage, that would rival any show on Broadway today. A few of those actors have gone on to star in broadway shows. I am happy to say that I have been blessed to perform in many shows at EPAC and also to direct both "Ten Little Indians", and the first dinner theatre for EPAC, "Bus Stop" held at the American Legion. At one time or another, I held all the offices on the board of directors except treasurer. After many years I felt that it was time for me to retire from the board and pass my chair on to the next generation.

There are only a few times in my life when I was truly surprised. One of those was the award dinner for the Ephrata Performing Arts Center, held at Doneckers Restaurant. What a fun and exciting night! I was awarded the very first "Lifetime Achievement Award," given by EPAC and couldn't believe this was happening to me. I was speechless! And for anyone who knows me, I'm never speechless! This was one of the most memorable moments of my life, to be honored with such an important award. I will never forget this fairytale event. Hard work does pay off!

Rainbow Dinner Theatre owners, David and Cynthia Di Savino were new to the area and had opened a new dinner theatre east of Lancaster. They saw me in the musical "Oliver" at EPAC and cast me in one of their shows, "Any Wednesday." This led to many more shows over the years and is also where I met my second husband, Ernie Young. Who knew, that someday I'd marry him? At the time I was married to Bill, but you never know how things will work out in a person's life. The places you go, the people you meet, they will all have an effect on your life in some way or another.

Today the playhouse in Ephrata is a beautiful state of the art facility. Back in the 70's and 80's there wasn't any air conditioning or heat in the building. You'd roast when it was above 80 degrees outside. We used to have matinees on

Saturday and the dressing rooms would easily reach 105 degrees . If you were doing a show wearing heavy coats and clothing it would be unbearable. We had a bathroom behind the stage, near the dressing rooms, but you couldn't flush the toilet while the show was going on, for fear the audience would hear it. That could break the mood of the show in an instant. You could hear the cars speeding by the theatre on their way to the swimming pool or the park. Finally the borough closed the road to thru traffic.

The only air we had flowing through, was by opening the windows on both sides, and we were lucky if we had a cross breeze. When the building was first built, it was a roller skating rink and then a dance hall. The roof also leaked and if it rained, we put buckets on the floor to catch the rain. We had dedicated community actors. They had day jobs and gave freely of their time for no pay. They loved acting and were passionate about what they were doing. That's what "amateur" means, for the love of it!

Today EPAC is open all year round. A few years ago the playhouse went through a multi-million dollar renovation. How proud I am of what this beautiful theatre has become. If you ever have an opportunity to attend a show at the theatre, you'll be glad you did! Why go to New York when you can come to Ephrata and see just as good! It's a lot less money too. The official name of the playhouse is now, The Ephrata Performing Arts Center at the Sharadin Bigler Theatre.

Dollie Fowler and Art High in Sly Fox at Rainbow Dinner Theatre Opening show in their new dinner theatre.

The Music Man, at the Ephrata Performing Arts Center. Dollie Fowler and Jeff Munro

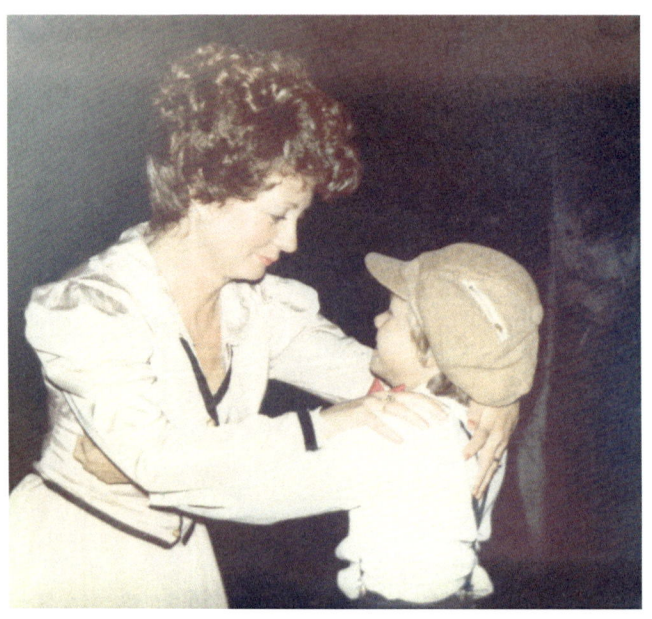

Dad, the Preachers' Son

Yes, dad was the son of a preacher. He had two brothers and four sisters. Grandpa Edds family was from Kentucky and Ohio. Grandpa Edds told me, his dad, my great grandpa, was the Mayor, Sheriff, and the undertaker of a small town, all at the same time. I found this very interesting, because my Grandpa was the Mayor, Preacher and Justice of Peace all at the same time.

Dad was very excited when we moved to Lancaster. He had been working with the Amish and Mennonite farmers in Pennsylvania for years. They purchased his stock conditioner, a feed additive that was fed to their animals and it did wonders for their health. Dad received letters of testimony from the farmers every week telling him how good his product was, and to please bring them more of the Edds Feed Supplement. Farmers all across the US and Canada fed the feed. This was my grandfather's secret recipe. I guess you could say he was one of the last medicine men. After all the ingredients were purchased, it was taken to a feed mill in Ohio, where it was mixed and then put in different size containers to be sold all across the country.

Dad knew all the plain farmers by name and where they lived without looking at the names on their mail boxes. It was a treat when dad stayed with us on his business trips. He always had so many good stories to tell us and was an excellent tour guide, dad taught me so much about the Amish and their customs.

When it was time for a meal at an Amish home, Dad was always invited to join the family. He made many plain friends over the years, and was always willing to give a helping hand when needed. During one of his visits to an amish farm, a plow horse came running into the barnyard dragging a young boy, who had gotten his foot caught in the harness. The boy was bleeding from numerous cuts and dad offered to drive the boy to the hospital, but not before the boy's mother could wash the blood from him and dress him with clean clothes. There were always so many stories, they could fill another book.

One day, Dad brought Grandma Edds for a visit, that's when I found out, my grandma was Pennsylvania Dutch. Her family was from this area of Lancaster county, so it's no wonder I loved this country so much. Grandma's family name is Stahl and Bailey, and they were from Marietta. What a surprise! This was the last trip Grandma Edds would ever make to Pennsylvania. She passed away after having her gall bladder removed at age 94. I learned a lot of new information about my ancestors during her visit.

Grandma was so hungry for fried chicken, but when she arrived at my house, I had made meatloaf, not knowing they had meatloaf for lunch on the turnpike. The next day Dad took grandma to one of the family style restaurants thinking they would have fried chicken, but they had meatloaf, ham and beef. So, the next day grandma made her own chicken pot pie. We all had a big laugh about the fried chicken and meatloaf, but at least she ate chicken the third day, even if she had to make it herself.

My family had such good times when dad worked in PA. One day we went bowling and Dad dropped a 16 pound bowling ball on his big toe. It turned black and blue, and very swollen and painful, he could hardly walk. Then there was the day he wanted me to color his hair, it was dark and had some gray, now it's called salt and pepper. He used to have black hair and very wavy. He thought it would be good to just put a little color on it. I told dad to just shampoo the dye in his hair and wait 20 minutes, then wash it out. He did what I ask him to do, but when I saw him a little later he said, "look at my hands, what should I do? I can't get this black dye off of my hands." He didn't wear the gloves that came with the dye and his hands turned jet black. It was so funny, I couldn't believe it. We scrubbed and washed his hands so much that evening that they were getting sore. Dad kept saying, "What are the Amish farmers going to say when they see me with black hands?" I told him to wear gloves. It took a couple days for dye to fade from his hands. Those were the days, I have many treasured memories. Many of these stories still give me a good laugh.

Dad remarried in the 70's to Alta. She was 10 years older, but that was not an issue and they were very happy for many years. They lived in Ohio in the spring and summer, and wintered in Florida the rest of the year. One year they couldn't go to Florida, because Dad had an aortic aneurism and needed surgery. He hated missing that year in Florida. A few years later their trip to Florida went as planned.

They had been at their Florida home for only a few days, when I received a phone call about midnight. The phone rang and rang. I looked at the clock and wondered who could be calling so late at night. It was my step-sister's husband, informing me that my dad and step-mother had been killed in a car wreck. I couldn't believe it! I remember saying," both of them?" I think I asked that question at least twice, I just couldn't believe it! I told myself, this was a bad dream, maybe I'll wake up. I cried and cried. How could my dad be dead? From a car wreck? To me, he was the best driver in the world. I was devastated!

A nineteen year old young man, driving a pickup truck, hit them broadside and killed them instantly. They didn't know what hit them. This was one of the saddest days of my life. I've read about families losing more than one family member at a time, and now I know how terrible it has to be for them.

We made the trip to Ohio for the double funeral. I was filled with so much grief. I think of my dad often and I miss him so much, and I still find myself telling stories about him from years ago. He had a great sense of humor, was a good singer and could play many instruments by ear. What wonderful memories to share with my family. It's important to keep those memories alive by passing them on to your family. Don't let them die!

My mom died a few years before my dad. She was in the bathtub taking a bath and just went to sleep. Her heart slowed down and just stopped. My step-dad found her in the tub, when he came home from work, and the water was still running. There was so much water everywhere. It had run all night and was running out the front door. This was a shock too, because my aunt (mom's sister) also died while taking a bath in the tub a few years earlier. Deep down, I knew my parents loved each other, they just couldn't live together. They divorced twice and remarried each other twice. Sometime in 1970 they got divorced for good.

Dad, Mom, Chris, Mark and Keith, when we livd in Farmingdale, NY.

Christina Lynn

Chris was born a few weeks early and weighed in at five pounds, with black curly hair that laid around her face in ringlets. She was a beautiful baby, so tiny and delicate. A perfect child growing up, never gave me any worries or problems. Music and singing was very important to her. One day I heard her singing in her bedroom and listened outside the door. She was singing a song from the movie, Mary Poppins, wearing her Easter bonnet and standing in front of the mirror singing her heart out. Chris was so cute and sang well, but her dreams of becoming a singer never quite developed.

Bill, bought Chris a yellow Camaro convertible for graduation. She was so proud of that car. One day as I backed down the driveway, I didn't look in my rear view mirror and hit the Camaro. Bang! I knocked her car out of the driveway into the street, the car started to roll down the road, jumping the curb, going through my yard and the neighbors, missing trees, and my only thought was to stop her car, before it went over a 10 foot embankment. I was running along beside the car, pulled open the drivers door, and jumped into the car and stepped on the emergency break just in the nick of time. I went into the house to tell Chris what had happened. She had her head phones on listening to music and didn't hear the crash. Chris screamed and went running outside, with no shoes on and there was snow on the ground. She never parked her car in the driveway, it was always parked on the street, so it was a real accident and by the time I had looked up, it was too late! We had her car repaired and it was as good as new. I felt so bad.

One day, she decided she wanted to go to Philadelphia to see the Michael Jackson concert, but couldn't find anyone to go with her. All of her friends said the tickets were too expensive, so she went by herself. Years had passed by before I found out about this! The thought of Chris as a teenager driving all the way to Philadelphia at night and alone, of course I would never have let her go. She has always been independent. If she wanted to do something she just did it. She started a full time job the Monday after she graduated from high school and couldn't wait to get her own apartment and be on her own.

Christina's Dad didn't live to see her get married in the coming fall. He would have been a very proud father, walking his daughter down the isle. A few years later, little Sabrina came into the world by C-section. Sabrina looked perfect, but she wasn't. I had a feeling there was a problem with the baby. The nurses said she could suck, but couldn't swallow. They had taken x-rays and test, but couldn't figure out what was wrong with her.

After I got home I couldn't get little Sabrina out of my mind, and couldn't sleep. The voice inside me kept saying, so back to the hospital! When I arrived the EMT'S were there preparing to take Sabrina to the Hershey Medical Center. So I rushed over to Hershey to be with Sabrina in place of my daughter, since she was a patient in the Lancaster Hospital. Sabrina's dad had been called and he was also on his way to Hershey. I didn't realize how fast I drove until I arrived at the hospital before the ambulance.

Hershey Hospital was the best place for Sabrina. The doctors ran test for 3 to 4 hours before telling us, that she was missing the aortic arch to her heart and also had 2 holes in her heart. We were in shock! What do we do now? Will she survive? I had so many questions for her doctors. We were told, that Sabrina was in the best hospital in the country for her medical problem. Hershey Medical Center was the hospital that perfected the aortic transplant surgery. Sabrina's chance of survival was 70% and the doctor said girls fight harder than boys, so this gave her an edge. We were definitely at the best hospital. Three days later Baby Sabrina had her open heart surgery. This was truly a miracle.

Sabrina was kept alive during the days before her surgery, by giving her a drug that comes from snake venom. The doctors gave her just enough to paralyze her and keep her from moving and waving her arms and legs around. By allowing this to happen, the small connection that kept Sabrina alive before she was born, would have dissolved.. After they are born, it's no longer needed and dissolves in a few days. The doctors had 3 days to get their surgical team together for Sabrina's open heart surgery.

My daughter, was still in the hospital in Lancaster, recovering from her C-section and my heart went out to Chris. She was weak from her surgery and couldn't travel to Hershey for Sabrina's open heart surgery. The surgery was successful, so it was a wonderful day for all the family. It just broke my heart to see a tiny baby in recovery, after an aortic transplant. A few days later we were told, Sabrina had a stroke during her surgery.

Sabrina was in the new neonatal unit for 6 weeks before she was allowed to come home. There was a problem getting Sabrina to swallow, and some of the doctors wanted to put in a feeding tube, but her pediatrician said she had had enough surgery and needed time to heal from all the trauma her body had suffered.

I went to the hospital during the day to help the nurses work with Sabrina's feedings, and Chris and Jay would arrive in the afternoon. Our little angel was getting most of her feedings through a tube in her nose. I'd work with her, giving Sabrina a bottle everyday, and finally she got the hang of sucking and swallowing. There were plenty of rocking chairs, so I would rock and sing to her every day. Babies love to be touched and held close. They can feel your love and will recover so much faster. You can never touch or hold a baby too much.

I ask her surgeon how serious her condition was and he said she might live to be 20 years old. This was a shock to me, I didn't expect to hear him say that! He said someday she would out grow the aortic arch and would need to have another transplant. Today Sabrina is 23 years old and has not had more surgery, except for a feeding tube a few years ago.

Most of her life she has been sick, with breathing and lung problems. Months of her life have been spent in and out of the hospital. There were times when she was on life support, but she has always pulled through. She is a strong willed young woman and has spent months of her life in the hospital. Sabrina is doing well and has a boyfriend even a job. I am so happy for her. It hasn't been easy for Christina. Chris has been a wonderful mother, with her daughter's needs always coming first. She was always taking time off work when Sabrina was a patient in the hospital and staying over night with her. There were times when Sabrina was a patient for over 4 weeks at a time.

Several years ago Chris and her husband got a divorce ,and they now share the care of Sabrina. A nurse comes to the house to spend the night with Sabrina just in case she has trouble with her breathing. She can be well one day and the next day very sick and not able to breath. She is a very delicate young woman today and has additional medical problems. Every day we have her on this earth is a very special blessing.

Christina and Sabrina

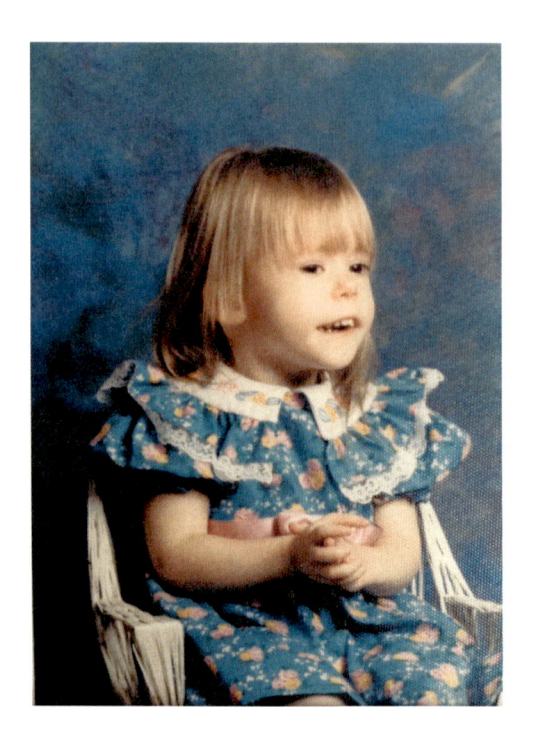

Mark, He Mark Gave His All

Mark entered the world on July 1, 1959 in Van Wert Ohio. I was sure he would be an Independence Day baby, born on July 4, but he was eager to enter the world a few days early. Maybe that's the reason he always liked fireworks. So, I thought I would walk to the hair dresser and get my hair shampooed. My stomach was large and it made it difficult for me to wash my own hair.

I was sitting under the hair dryer when I started to have labor pains. My contractions were about 5 minutes apart. The hair dresser was combing my hair when I told her I was in labor. She wanted to call someone for me, but I refused and said there was plenty of time before the baby arrived. Walking home, it was such a beautiful day. With my first child I was in labor for 22 hours, so of course, I thought I had plenty of time.

During the walk home I had some very hard contractions. They were so hard I had to stop walking and was doubled over in pain until they subsided. I finally made it home and called Bill to take me to the hospital. He arrived and we made it to the hospital in just a few minutes,since we lived only a few blocks away. While Bill was downstairs filling out admission papers before he came up to the delivery room, I had delivered Mark. I couldn't get over how fast the delivery was. I think this was because I was so relaxed by the walking and having my hair done.

Three years later we moved to Warsaw, Indiana. Mark was a curious child, and always getting into something. One morning he came into our bedroom about 5am and said, "Mommy, I've had my breakfast." I looked at the clock and told him to get in bed with us, it was too early to get up. A few seconds passed and I started to smell something that smelled like oranges. I jumped up and ask Mark what he had said and again he said, he had breakfast. Right away, I knew he had somehow reached the child vitamins from the top shelve of the cupboard and eaten them, but how could he reach them, they were up so high? I ran to the kitchen and I saw where he had pushed a chair up to the counter, stood on the chair, climbed up on the counter and used the shelves as a ladder to climb and get the vitamins. He also ate baby aspirin that was flavored orange. What a mess in the kitchen. He had tried to play with some of the pills by putting them in pop bottles, so I wasn't sure just how many he had eaten.

I woke Bill and told him what Mark had done and then I called the doctor. The doctor said to take him to the hospital

ASAP and he would meet us there. Mark had his stomach pumped and the doctor said he would probably sleep the rest of the day and not to worry, but he would be fine. It was a rainy day and Mark loved to walk in the rain, so I stopped at my favorite shoe store and bought him a pair of boots. He jumped in every puddle he could find that day, and never took a nap!

By the time he started in kindergarten, we had moved to the country. Mark took the school bus to school with his sister. One day after school, Mark didn't come home. Chris got off the bus but there was not Mark. I called the school and was told the bus driver had seen him on the bus. Where was he, what had happened to him?

I decided to walk over to the neighbor's and see if her children had seen Mark. He always liked to play at their house, because their son had fun toys that were different then Mark's. I knocked on the door, the mother came to the door, and gave me a very unwelcoming look. I asked if they had seen Mark and told her what happened and she told me that Mark got off the school bus at her house and said I had told him to stay and play with her son after school. Well, of course none of this was true. He just wanted to play with some new toys. Yes, I was mad! I thought someone had kidnapped him or he had drowned in the pond. He was all Boy, never a dull moment.

The years continued to fly by. I'm sure many people ask themselves where the years have gone. It seems like the older you get the faster they go. Mark was 11 years old when we moved to Akron, PA. in Lancaster County- Amish Country. It is one of the most beautiful places in the world. I consider Lancaster County my home. I had just turned thirty years old when I moved to Pennsylvania, and I have lived here for over 40 years,

Grandpa Fowler, taught Mark to fish before he started school. He developed his talents as an expert by reading all the sports magazines he could get his hands on. His favorite was fly fishing, but he loved all types of fishing. There's nothing like having fresh trout for dinner.

Mark played baseball on Little League, was a Boy Scout, finished his Eagle badge, but never got the Eagle award, because he had turned 18, became assistant scout master, had a paper route at 11 and was involved in sports. My son loved life, was happy, and had many friends. In Junior High Mark started to play football. He was very good and played all through high school. He lettered in three sports, baseball, football and wrestling. However, the sport that he excelled in was wrestling. His coach said he was an unorthodox wrestler, In other words, he had his own style and way of doing things. I think this made it more difficult for his opponents. Mark was team captain and set a new pin record at Ephrata High School. A few years later another young man came along and set a new pin record.

I would get so nervous when I'd attend his wresting matches. My heart would feel like it was going to jump out of my body and my stomach would hurt so bad that I could hardly stand it. Once Mark's match was over, all the stress and pain would stop. Wrestling gave me an ulcer. Can you believe that? The doctor told me that maybe I should skip going to his matches, but we decided that it would be worse for me to not attend. So I continued to go and I was happy to watch him. The pain was worth it. Mark liked to go for the pin right away, go for the kill as they say, get it over with fast. There was a time in my life when I thought I would like to be the first female referee for wrestling. The referees made so many wrong calls, I thought I could do a better job. I guess we all think that when we're watching a sporting match, that we could do it better, when in truth, we couldn't. I'm proud to say that I did not miss any of my son's sporting events while he was in school.

Late in his senior school year, Mark skipped school a day to travel to Harrisburg and visit an Army recruiter. I didn't know anything about this until he returned home and showed me the papers he had signed. Bill knew Mark was going to sign up for the Army, but they both thought it best not to tell me until it had been done. He had arranged to enter the Army soon after he graduated from high school. I was shocked! I couldn't believe it! My knees seemed to grow very weak and I felt like I'd pass out. He was 18, so there was nothing I could do about it. Mark wanted to be an Air Borne Ranger in Special Forces and by signing up early, the Army promised that when an opening became available for Ranger

School, he would have his chance. One day his dream finally came true.

Mark had only been out of high school a few weeks when he left home for basic training in New Jersey. The day he left, I cried like a baby, I couldn't help myself. The feeling I had in my heart and soul was one that a mother should never have to experience. I knew things would never be the same from that day forward, but I didn't know why. His basic training was still close enough to home, that we were able to visit a few times before he flew off to infantry school, then airborne school and after that, Fort Lewis, Washington, to await his opportunity to enter Ranger school.

The United States Army Ranger School is an intense 61-day combat leadership course oriented toward small-unit tactics. It has been called the "toughest combat course in the world" and "is the most physically and mentally demanding leadership school the Army has to offer."

I was proud and so happy for Mark. His dream was coming true. What mother wouldn't be proud? Mark had gone through four schools in less than one year. He was one of the special few. The physical strength, power, mental intelligence and endurance that it takes to survive ranger school is a feat in itself. Only about 50% who are assigned to the school become Rangers. They just can't handle the physical endurance and the toll that it takes on your body. When he came home, after graduating ranger school, he had lost weight and was so pale. I asked him to tell me some of the things that happened to him. Mark said they had very little sleep, maybe a few hours a night, and survived on very little food. When you're in a real war and responsible for other mens safety, a Ranger has to know that he can be a leader, because his men are counting on him to keep them safe and make the correct decisions.

 He was in the mountain phase, very sleepy and hallucinating, when he thought he saw a tree and instead of leaves on the tree, it was a money tree. Mark fell off the edge of a mountain and suffered cuts, but he didn't quit. He most definitely was not a quitter. Altogether there are three phases of ranger school. You must make it through all three of those phases to pass and graduate. Mark came home for a few days before he was due back at Fort Lewis. He celebrated his 20 birthday with his family.

When he graduated from airborne school, which was before Ranger school, he ask me to fly to Fort Benning, GA. to attend his graduation. I was so proud to see my son jump from an airplane with the other soldiers who were graduating with him. The sky was filled with parachutes, opening one by one and flying through the air until they hit the ground. What a glorious sight!

Billy, Mark's little brother, wanted a uniform just like his big brother's, so Mark had one made for him, with all the army patches, airborne, his name. It was just like big brother's. Billy loved that uniform, it was so special to him.

Billy and I traveled to Fort Lewis to visit Mark. It was exciting to see where he was stationed and meet some of his friends. I am so thankful we made that trip. The weather was cool and crisp, just perfect for a fall day. We had a fantastic time with Mark and got to do a little sight seeing. We had dinner in the Space Needle, and stayed at a hotel right on the Puget Sound and Billy could open the window and fish right out the window. It was so much fun, but we didn't catch any fish. Finally it was time to say goodbye to Mark and drive him back to the base. I was so proud of him and all his accomplishments.

Billy and I were up early for our flight home the next morning. I had an uneasy feeling in the pit of my stomach, but I couldn't put my finger on it, so I just pushed it out of my mind. Mother's will understand what I'm talking about. I was so happy we had made the trip to see Mark.. Billy couldn't wait until he got home, so he could attend school and tell his friends about his brother, the Ranger, and his trip to Fort Lewis.

Mark and I always talked on the phone every other Sunday evening. We would take turns calling each other. One Sunday I waited and waited for him to call, since it was his turn, but there was no phone call. I was worried that something had happened, but his dad said I shouldn't worry and Mark was fine. I really wanted to pick up that phone and call him, but I wouldn't let myself. We had been told, that a Ranger had to have his equipment packed and ready to move out at moments notice, so I figured he was on an assignment. I had very little sleep that night, I just knew something was wrong.

Early the next morning, Billy and I were on a plane flying to Ohio to visit my family. Bill drove us to the Harrisburg airport ,and Billy was wearing the Army uniform that Mark had made for him. The pilot and attendants all commented on his uniform, and he was so proud to tell them that it was just like his big brother's. We had a good flight to Toledo, and my sister Billie and her husband Larry met us at the airport. It was a beautiful day, so we decided to stop and have lunch on the way to my sisters home in Defiance, Ohio. We were having such a good time visiting and catching up on all the news without a care in the world.

When we arrived at my sister's house, I noticed many cars in the driveway. There was my dad and step mother, mom and my step dad, my brother, cousins and a few other people. I thought they were all there to welcome us home. Boy was I wrong! I was totally blindsided and was not prepared for what I heard in the next few seconds.

I was walking up the driveway to the side door of the house, when my brother Jerry, came outside walking towards me. I was very happy to see him. He put his arms around me and hugged me. Jerry held on to me very tight for a number of seconds and whispered something in my ear. I pushed him back and said, what did you say? He told me the same thing again. Dollie…..Mark's dead! I pushed him back again and he put his arms around me and told me once more, Dollie,

Mark's dead! I couldn't believe my ears. You hear people talk about shock, well I was in the deepest shock of my life. My knees buckled, I could hardly stand up. How could this be true? My wonderful son that everyone loved, was dead? How could this have happened? I didn't believe it. Then I looked at Jerry's face and I knew it was true. I had never seen my brother cry before. Oh dear God, what am I going to do? This couldn't be happening to me. There has to be some mistake.

I was stunned as I walked into the house, went into a bedroom and shut the door. I cried my eyes out, it seemed like I cried for hours. Thoughts were racing though my head. I told myself, "Mark's not dead, the army has made a mistake, it's not Mark, it's someone else." My eyes and face were so swollen that I could hardly see. I knew I had to pull myself together and talk to my family, who were all waiting to talk to me, and then I thought, what is my little ten year old son thinking? My heart went out to little Billy and what he must be thinking. I just wanted to make him feel better and not hurt so much, and then I thought of Bill and Chris, at home. I felt like my life was ending. You ask yourself, why me? Why did two of my sons have to die? Why not someone else? It just didn't seem fair. Why wasn't the hurt and pain spread around a little? It just didn't seem fair that I had lost two children and some people go through life and nothing ever happens to their families. I was having a difficult time getting my head around this. I wanted to scream, maybe I should have. The thought that came into my mind, was the Kennedy family and all the deaths their family had endured over the years.

God must have had a reason for choosing me for all the heartache in my life. I wondered what that reason must be. Why me? I had to pick myself up, put on a happy face, and go on, even though I was hurting so very badly, with all my heart. I still had a husband and two children depending on me. Life goes on, I will survive.

The phone rang and it was Bill. He wanted me to wait and fly home the next day, but I wanted to head back to the airport and catch the next flight for Harrisburg. I just wanted to go home with my young son. My brother and sister flew home with me. They didn't want me to go alone. I did so much thinking on that flight home, about my daughter, Chris, how was she feeling, I couldn't wait to get back home to her.

I sat with my arm around Billy most of the flight home. He said very little and was still wearing the uniform his brother gave him. I talked to him about what had happened, but there wasn't much I could say to a 10 year old, but tell him that I loved him. He looked so sad and my heart was breaking for him.

Bill was the type man who kept everything inside, so you never knew what he was thinking. When he met us at the airport he had someone else driving the car. I think he picked Billy up and carried him to the car. He had his arm around me most of the way home, but we said very little. What could we say? Our son was dead! What happened? We had so many questions, but nothing would bring him back to us.

The Army notified Bill first. He had returned to work, after driving us to the airport and was walking past the front door of his business on Harrisburg Pike, when he saw two military officers coming up the walk towards the front door. He said, the minute he saw them, he knew what had happened. He just knew! Bill was right, they had come to give us the terrible news of our son's unexpected death.

TV stations had been calling us and wanted an interview. I was so devastated, how could I speak to someone from a TV station? I refused all of their calls. Looking back, I wish I would have spoken to them, but that's hindsight. Some of the information in the paper was also wrong. I was told by friends, that the news of Mark's death even made the newspaper in North Carolina.

We had wonderful friends and relatives who rallied around us. With their support we managed to get through the awful days ahead. It always helps to talk to friends and not keep it bottled up inside. Bill had a difficult time discussing what happened. He wouldn't even talk to me about it. This was his personality, he always kept everything trapped inside.

Bill made most of the funeral arrangements with the Stradling funeral home. There wasn't much we needed to do, since the Army had chosen the casket. All we had to do was wait for our son's body to arrive at the airport and home. The

Army asked me if there was anything they could do for me, and I requested that they permit a close friend of Mark's to come home with him. Dennis Strohm was in the Army stationed in Alaska, but he was given leave to come home.

Mark died on August 12 and his funeral was on the 18 of August. Before the Army released his body, they held a service for Mark at Fort Lewis, and Dennis Strohm, Mark's best friend, was there for the service. I wanted to attend, but Bill thought I should stay home. We had relatives coming in for the funeral, but my heart was in Fort Lewis with Mark.

The next week was a big blur for me. I don't know who I saw or spoke to. All I know is that there were many people around me. Everywhere I looked there were people. The question that people always seem to ask is, "how are you doing?" Well, for sure, you're not good, but you pretend you're fine. That's the worst question to ask a person who has just lost a loved one. They all wanted to help in some way, but there was really nothing they could do, except just be there for you and don't be afraid to talk about what's happened. Nobody could bring my son back to me. I was still in shock. Every song you hear has a new meaning for you, it's like the words were written just for you. I cried and cried and cried. I was so sad, a part of me was missing, forever.

The day before the funeral, as I was looking at Mark in his casket, I thought, that's not Mark, it's a wax figure that looks like him. You try to tell yourself all kinds of things that you know are not true, because you don't want to believe your son is really dead and in that casket. You are in total denial and believe he is still alive, probably on a special mission for the Army. After all, he was a Ranger in Special Forces, and many of their missions were top secret.

The church was overflowing and people were standing in the back. My friend, Jacqueline Rupp, played the piano for the service, such a wonderful pianist. I wanted to include many of the songs Mark loved. One of my favorite songs, "The Wind Beneath My Wings" by Larry Gavin, was a song I choose for Mark. The words had such meaning for me, "fly high like an eagle". I could just see Mark flying in the sky, he loved the outdoors. Mark's service was very special. The wrestling coach, Mervin Witmer and Captain James Towns III, gave the memorial eulogies. They captured Mark's character so well. It was perfect, and I was so proud of my son.

The Rev. Denton L. Spencer, officiated the service and I feel I must share a few of his comments with you. "Death is a great receiver, it turns out some lights and it turns on others. Extinguished today is the light of joy and cheer that flashed from his eyes, but turned on is the light of record and character of him who is gone. When we look back at someone like Mark for instance, with a zest for life, as he had it, who attained, by shear courage and determination, a great portion of his dreams and goals at so young an age, our sense of wonder grows that such a young man was among us for a short while, and so many never knew that one of his caliber was here. I believe today we are commemorating the life of a young man who looks larger in his death (as we look back) then when he walked among us.

His course of life ran out so soon. It all happened so suddenly before he ever reached the prime of life. We'll never come to know, in this world , the influence and usefulness to which Mark one day would have attained. Who can understand or explain such a sudden halting of a life so promising as his, but the Eternal One Himself, into whose merciful and loving presence Mark has so quickly passed to render his account of faithfulness. His sportsmanship and good humor brought joy to his loved ones and inspired the admiration of his friends.

The following is a letter from one of Marks school friends who was serving in the Navy:

Dear Mr. & Mrs. Fowler,

It grieves me very much to write this letter. I never thought I'd be writing a letter like this. I learned about your sons death on the 20th of this month when I received a letter from my mother with the news papers clipping of the accident. When I received the letter, I don't mind telling you I cried. I know Mark from school, he was a school mate , but also a good friend. So now I send you my deepest regrets. I know I can't imagine the grief your going through, but I know it couldn't be touched by anything.

I'm very sorry,

Seaman Recruit.............

A beautiful letter from a young man who has so much insight and deep feelings in his soul. I will cherish this letter forever.

A letter from one of Marks teachers.

> Dear Mr. and Mrs. Fowler,
>
> My sympathy is with you, my thoughts and prayers too, as you go through this difficult time. I was shocked to hear of the death of Mark, and thought at that moment that the world and you lost a light and a smile that can never be replaced.
>
> I was Mark's homeroom teacher for four years at Ephrata. I also had him in an English class. He was a good boy with a ready smile and he always could tell good, funny stories. There were times when he would keep the homeroom listening for almost a whole period. Once he told me the story of the rabbit, when he was hunting, that jumped up and bit him in the stomach. I had a feeling maybe he was pulling my leg. But he had a great sense of humor.
>
> His death is a terrible loss for you. I pray friends and family and beautiful memories of Mark will help through this time.
>
> I know I hold good memories of him in his high school days.
>
> May God be with you.
>
> Sincerely,
>
> Judith H.

The Honor Guard was at the cemetery when we arrived, and were in full dress uniform. They looked so special and young. I was told they were young men still on active duty and not retired soldiers. When there is a military funeral, they usually have retired soldiers as the honor guard. My dad, who was a WWII veteran told me Marks funeral was the most impressive military funeral that he had ever attended. He was very impressed with every aspect of the service. When I heard the 21 gun salute and taps, I thought, this was the end, final, it was over! To this day, I still tear up when I hear taps.

Isn't it amazing how a person's mind can play tricks? I'd be home alone, and sometimes I would hear the floor in the attic creek and other sounds, like someone walking. I'd think, Mark is home, he's come back and he's in the attic. He used to spend time in the attic, it was like a man cave would be today, and he kept many of his personal items up there. I do believe his spirit was in our house. Was he letting me know, that he was all right?

I knew I had to continue with my life, there was a house to run, a family to care for, a young son, food to buy, so many things to do. The first time I went to the grocery store after the funeral, I was hurt by how people treated me. One couple saw me in the aisle and quickly moved their cart to another aisle where I couldn't see them. I figured they didn't know what to say to me, so they just wanted to avoid me. Well, I wasn't going to let this happen. I didn't know if they knew about Mark, and I wanted to find out. I approached them and they didn't mention Mark, so I asked if they knew he had died. They said yes, but they didn't know what to say to me, so they just thought they would avoid me. Let me tell you, that's the wrong thing to do. Please don't ever do that to someone you know. They don't deserve to be ignored. People just don't know what to say to another person when someone dies. It's very easy, just tell them you know and you're sorry for their loss. That's all, you don't need to say more.

People have asked me over the years which was the worse shock for me, having a son die of a chronic illness or getting the news about the death of a child without any warning. I can only tell you how I felt with each of these events. Of course, when a loved one is ill you always believe they are the one who is going to beat the odds and survive. When they're sick for months and sometimes years, even though you pray your loved on will live, and you are sure they will, deep down in your gut, you are preparing yourself for the inevitable. When you receive news that your child has been killed or died, with no warning, right out of the blue, you are in total shock. Nothing in this world can prepare you for the news you have just heard. Nothing!

I prayed and prayed to God to help me get through this awful time. I asked myself, why me, why me? What did I do to deserve this? My heart is breaking. I tried to pull myself together for my family. I thought of my children and what they must be going through. I wonder if people think about the children, and what they're thinking when something like this happens in a family. Don't forget the children. Talk to them about their feelings, listen to them. They're hurting too.

We asked for donations to be made in Mark's name for a memorial fund, to the Ephrata Recreation Center. Later in the year we were able to buy uniforms with some of the funds for the wrestling team at the recreation center. The team didn't have uniforms, and it was wonderful to see that all the young men on the team had matching uniforms when they participated in a team sport. Young Billy was so proud of those gold and purple uniforms. I think the new uniforms gave the young men pride, honor and helped them win many matches through out the season.

Days after everything was over and we were trying to get back to normal, the door bell rang. I wondered who could be at the door so early in the morning sinceI wasn't expecting anyone. I opened the door, looked at the man standing in front of me, and we both threw our arms around each other and cried. It was one of the wrestling coaches, Phil Muth. He said he was on vacation when he received the news about Mark, and couldn't continue with his trip knowing what had happened, he had to come home right away. Phil drove straight through the night from New England and didn't stop until he arrived at my house early the next morning. Mark thought the world of his wrestling coaches, Mervin Witmer and Phil Muth. Mark held the pin record at Ephrata High School in wrestling for many years. A year later the coaches gave the Mark Fowler award in wrestling to a wrestler who had given more then 100% of himself though out the wrestling season. I was thrilled that the team honored Mark with such a special award. To me this was special, because a younger wrestler could earn this award, and didn't have to be on the varsity team.

How did my son die? What caused his death? I will try to answer these questions and hope you will understand them, because I don't. I'll start by saying the Army has told us many different stories, official records, death records, letters from Washington DC, they all say something different.

The Army told us, Mark died from a gunshot wound to the back of the head. There was no live ammunition allowed in the Ranger living quarters, so the Army tells us. This accident (they say) happened in the Ranger barracks. The Army said, " Mark was holding the gun when it misfired." These facts can't be true. Mark did not have any gunpowder residue on his hands. He was left handed, so how could he have been holding the gun, fire it, and shoot himself in the back of the head, on the left side? There was not an entry wound in the front of his head. One of the Rangers told us he was standing near his locker when it fired. We had been told that a group of soldiers had been playing with the gun and they put one bullet inside the chamber. It was the wrong size, so they thought it wouldn't fire, but It did fire, killing Mark. My husband went to a firing range to shoot a 357 magnum with the same size bullet, he fired at least 100 rounds, and the gun wouldn't fire.

Mark, was an expert in handing firearms. Doc Herr, who was an avid hunter and a very close family friend, told us that he knew Mark very well, and there's no way, he could have been holding the gun when it fired. Mark and Doc did a lot of hunting together over the years. I've heard many more stories very similar to this one and how safe Mark was with guns.

This past year, I again went through all the official papers from the Army, concerning Marks death and found many inconsistencies. One document said he died in the p.m. and another said he died in the a.m. I went to Ft. Lewis in August of 2013 to get some answers. The CID (criminal investigation department) at the base helped me fill out papers, from the " Freedom of Information Act", to get Mark's files and records. The detective even faxed the papers to D.C. for me. The CID checked their files and had no record of ever investigating Mark's death at Ft. Lewis. He said his office was not notified.

 A few weeks later I received a letter from the Army, which said Mark's records were not available to me. Why wouldn't they release my sons records? What were they hiding? Where was he when he was shot? I am so upset over this and have written other letters and can't get any answers. I just want to know what really happened to my son!

Many years have gone by since Mark's death, but I can't close the door on what happened to him. Am I wrong to want answers? This has dug at my soul for years and I just can't put it to rest. Is it too much to want to know the truth?

Ranger Creed

<u>Recognizing</u> that I volunteered as a Ranger, fully knowing the hazards of my choose profession, I will always endeavor to uphold the prestige, honor, and high esprit do corps of my Ranger Regiment.

<u>Acknowledging</u> the fact that a Ranger is more elite soldier who arrives at the cutting edge of battle by land, sea, or air, I accept the fact that as a Ranger my country expects me to move further, faster and fight harder than any other soldier.

<u>Never</u> shall I fail my comrades. I will always keep myself mentally alert, physically strong and morally straight and I

will shoulder more than my share of the task whatever it may be and, one hundred percent and then some.

Gallantly will I show the world that I am a specially selected and well trained soldier. My courtesy to superior officers, neatness of dress and care of equipment shall set the example for others to follow.

Energetically will I meet the enemies of my country. I shall decent them on the field of battle for I am better trained and will fight with all my might. Surrender is not a Ranger word. I will never leave a fallen comrade to fall into the hands of the enemy and under on circumstances will I ever embarrass my country.

Readily will I display the intestinal fortitude required to fight on to the Ranger objective and complete the mission, though I be the lone surviver.

RANGERS LEAD THE WAY

Mark's life came to a end on August 12, 1979. He loved life, but it ended all to soon.

Mark above and picture below jumping from a plane.

Bill

We had ups and downs in our marriage like any normal couple. There wasn't a lot of communication, since Bill wasn't a talker, at least when he was home. Bill loved to read novels and probably read at least one or two books a week. He was an excellent provider and very good at his profession, as a photo engraver. In the late 70's he started a new business and was very successful. He was kind, a very giving man and would have given you his last dollar. He didn't know how to say no to anyone.

The years continued to pass very quickly. Bill spent much of his time away from home and in bars drinking with other business men. We were lucky if he was home one or two nights during the week, for dinner with the family.

After Mark died, he tried his best to help his family get over our loss. About a week after Mark's funeral, Bill came home with our motor home and told us he wanted to take Billy and me to Niagara Falls for a few days. He though it would somehow make me feel better. Nothing could help me with the great loss I felt over losing my son. I thought about him day and night. You blame yourself and all kinds of things go through your mind, and you ask yourself, what if I had done this, and what if I had done that, maybe he would still be alive, just trying to make some sense of what had happened. Every song I heard on the radio had a new meaning for me. It's as if you're hearing it for the first time. I cried so much, I couldn't help myself. Oh how I missed Mark with all my heart! I didn't want to go on a trip, but I knew Bill needed this for himself, so we traveled to Niagara Falls.

We had friends living on the American side of the Falls and they wanted us to visit them. They used to be our neighbors in Akron and it would be so nice to see them again. Billy was happy to go on the trip. He was 11 now and very excited to travel in a motorhome, with all the comforts of home. Chris stayed home, since she had a full time job. She loved working and being on her own.

We arrived at our friends' house and parked the motor home in their driveway. Visiting with friends helped me take my mind off how sad I was and we all had a very pleasant evening. Early the next morning, we drove across the border. This was the first time we had never been to the Canadian side of Niagara Falls. The Falls were so beautiful and we had a wonderful day, doing all the things a tourist would do. When our day was over, we stopped and got my friend a beautiful arrangement of flowers and I was so eager to give them to her.

We were running low on fuel, so Bill thought we'd fill up with gas on the Canadian side before crossing into New York. The gas was cheaper in Canada. A motor home takes many gallons of fuel to fill the tank. After Bill climbed in to the driver's seat, I told him I could smell gas and not to light a cigarette. He could smell it too and knew something was wrong. The smell was very strong and I was afraid we would blow up. We opened windows to get the gas smell out and drove to the border crossing.

The border police said I couldn't enter the United States with my flowers, because it was a live plant, and wasn't allowed. They took my beautiful arrangement and told us we could continue. I was so upset over this, because I should have known better. There would be no flowers for my friend.

When we got back to our friend's house, Bill and Carl checked for the gas leak and repaired it. I later wanted to take a shower in the motor home, so Bill went out to light the water heater. The moment he lit the match, there was an explosion. The whole house rocked, it was like a bomb had hit us. We all ran outside to see what had happened and couldn't believe our eyes.

It's a good thing Bill left the door open, because the explosion blew him right out the door. The windows blew out, the sides were bowed out, it was destroyed. Bill smelled like a burnt chicken. His hair, eyebrows, eyelashes, face and skin were burned and he was in pain. We took him to the hospital for treatment and then went out for dinner. I knew Bill was hurting and we all felt so bad for him, but we were so thankful he wasn't seriously hurt. The ER doctor said it was a wonder the explosion didn't kill him, and it would have if the door had been closed. The next morning we rented a car and drove home. Billy was so excited, because his dad let him pick out the rental car. He choose a camero. The car didn't have much room for everything we had to take home with us, items from inside the motor home, but we made it work with Billy just sat on top of things in the back seat. He was a happy to be riding in a camero and to hear Billy tell it, his dad raced all the way home.

When December came around, Bill wanted the family to go on a cruise. He knew this was something I always wanted to do, and of course he was still trying to help me feel better and not be so sad. So, we all went on a 7 day cruise and had a good time. I was so happy to see my children enjoying themselves and I must admit it was good for the whole family.

The years flew by and Bill and I didn't talk much about Mark, I wanted to, but he didn't. I think Bill was drinking more and smoked about 3 packs of cigarettes a day. We never had any liquor in the house, he did all his drinking with business associates away from home.

 Mark had bought a truck a few months before he died. The Army shipped his truck home and I enjoyed driving it, because it had belonged to my son. I felt such a connection with him when I was in the drivers seat. I could feel his presence. Bill didn't like seeing it in the driveway and asked me to sell the truck. I didn't want to, but for Bill's sake I sold the truck.

I knew Bill had health issues. You can't be married to a man for over 25 years and not know that your husband has a health problem. During the early 80's he had open heart surgery in Philadelphia, a triple bypass. This didn't surprise me one bit. I would drive the 60 miles each way every day to visit him. I thought finally he would see the light and stop his smoking. Boy, was I wrong!

One day as I was getting off the elevator in the hospital, the doors opened and there he stood, smoking a cigarette. I was in shock! How could he? Bill paid someone to buy him cigarettes and hid them behind the picture next to the elevator. The shock of seeing him smoking was more then I could bear. I couldn't even look at him, so I went home. I couldn't talk to him after seeing him smoking and it was only a few days after his open heart surgery.

Bill continued to abuse his body and was back in the hospital a few more times. He even had a pacemaker but when it was time to have it checked by phone, he wouldn't do it. The heart doctor told him that he had a death wish. I think the doctor was right.

Bill was very successful in business. He had more than half of his life before him and threw it all away. I know he was looking forward to grandchildren and retirement, but somehow he couldn't rise above losing two sons. I think the doctor was correct about his having a death wish.

The death wish won! Bill died April 30, 1987 of a heart attack while sleeping. He was 47 years old. What a waste, this didn't need to happen. The coroner said, "He died very peacefully and never knew what happened. His heart just blew out." He also told me, that Bill had had two previous heart attacks, but he had paid no attention to them. The dark areas of the heart show where the heart attacks occurred.

One day, I returned home from a performance at Rainbow Dinner Theatre and Billy was waiting for me. He told me to call our business, 'Dollie's In" right away, but our friend wouldn't tell Billy what was wrong. He said come over to the Tavern now! And don't ask any questions, just get here!!! I wondered what was wrong, what had happened? When we arrived I saw police cars and my heart was pounding. I was a wreck! I saw Bill's car parked in the parking lot and instantly thought something had happened to him. I thought maybe he had been robbed or shot. When he didn't open the tavern at 11 am like planned, many of the customers began to worry. Our friend used his key to go inside. He went upstairs and found Bill. He had a heart attack while sleeping. The police were there, because it was a place of business and someone had died inside. Bill just went to sleep and didn't wake up. The doctor said his heart blew out. He'd had a myocardial infarction and it killed him instantly.

Billy had just turned eighteen in March and this happened on April 30. Another blow for the family. How much can one family take? Now I had two children without a father

We all missed Bill. He missed his daughter Christina's wedding in September and wasn't here for the birth of his first grandchild. What a shame, because he would have been so in love with baby Shanelle. The choices we make today, will affect us for the rest of our lives. When a tragedy strikes, it's easy for a person to say that they're going to make a change in their life. They'll never take dangerous chances, pray and go to church more, be kind and live life like it's their last day on earth. How soon we all forget the promises we have made to ourselves.

Bill had sold his graphic arts business a few months before he died. I believe he knew that he didn't have long to live. Years later, I realized he tried to protect me by keeping things from me about his health. I was always the last to know.

I laid Bill to rest next to our son, Mark. They would keep each other company. Remember, how important it is, to live each day to the fullest. Oh, how we forget all too soon and take life for granted.

Billy

Billy was 14 months old when we moved to Akron, just walking and getting into everything. He was a beautiful baby with light red hair that turned blonde during his second year. With Chris and Mark in school all day, it was a joy to have my young son home with me. I tried not to spoil him, he was a blessing to me and I loved him very much.

After Billy was born, Bill's imagination was running away with him. One day he said, he thought Keith had been reincarnated and that Billy was really Keith. I knew he didn't believe this, but it made him feel better to think it was possible.

Billy finally started kindergarten and he was so eager. One of his teachers told me, he was so sweet, that she could just take him home with her. I wonder who he got his charm from? When the weather turned cool, I dressed him in a long sleeve shirt and when it turned warm he wore a short sleeve shirt to school. When he came home, he told me he couldn't wear a short sleeve shirt to school again, because he couldn't wipe his nose on his sleeve. He had been wiping his nose on his arm. I had a good laugh over that story.

Billy idolized his big brother. At times, Mark would take him along with him to movies, taught him to fish and took him visiting with his friends. When Mark went into the Army, Billy asked him for a uniform like the one he wore. So, after Mark graduated from Jump School, as a paratrooper, he had a uniform made for Billy, just like the one he wore. Billy loved wearing it and was so proud of his brother.

I called Billy my little man, because he loved to get dressed up and go out to eat. One day we were in New York City for a few days and went out to eat at a fancy French restaurant. People were looking at him and whispering when we walked in, thinking a young child shouldn't be brought into an upscale French restaurant to eat. It didn't take him long to impress the other guest. And many people commented on his manners and how handsome and well behaved he was. To this day he is still very charming.

The years continued to fly by and Billy got involved in wrestling, just like his brother. He was about seven when he started the sport and was 12 when he won third place in the Middle Atlantic State Tournament. I don't think I ever saw his dad jump so high as when Billy pinned his opponent. Later Bill and Billy made a trip to the World's Fair, just the two of them. It was a chance to become closer to each other.

After Mark died, it seemed like Billy lost interest in so much. I didn't know that he was having such problems. One day I was cleaning his bedroom and stuffed in the corner of his closet, I found the Army uniform that his brother had made for him and it was all cut up. I was stunned and wondered why he had done this! I thought, maybe it was because his brother was gone, so he didn't want the uniform anymore. Maybe cutting it up made Billy feel better. Sometimes a child will seem normal, but will start acting up in other ways. When he was in seventh grade, he started to hang out with an older group of kids. His grades dropped and he just wasn't himself; however, he put up a good front with his dad and me. The next year I sent him to a private school, but that didn't help. There was a certain group of young people, who were older and preyed on younger one's who were having problems. They did this for all the wrong reasons, hoping to get them involved with drugs. We needed to get him away from these people and out of the area right away, so we sent him to Ohio to live with my brother and go to school with his children. After a year in Ohio we thought if was safe to bring Billy home, but he still had problems to deal with. We were helping him as much as we could, but as a parent you question yourself so much. Are you doing the best for your child, is there anything you could have done, but didn't? So many questions.

When Billy was eighteen and his girl friend was sixteen, they ran away together. Her mother and I looked everywhere for them. I thought maybe they had gone to the shore. We used to rent a house for the summer in Wildwood, NJ, so I searched there and every where else I could think of, but we couldn't find them. Bill had died three months earlier, so I was on my own trying to find him. Finally his girlfriends mother found them. They were in Wildwood after all. We brought them home and they insisted they wanted to live together, and if we didn't let them, they would run away again. So, what does a parent do? We didn't want them to run away again, so we let them live together. Billy, found himself a good job locally, detailing custom vans. It was perfect for him and he really liked the work.

We were told they were expecting a baby in March. I was thrilled! I knew they were both young, but I had faith in them. Shanelle who was born March 21, weighed about 4 pounds, had beautiful black hair and an angel face. When the nurse brought her out for the family to see, her head was so small, it fit in the nurse's hand with space left over. Shanelle spent time in the hospital and came home on Easter Sunday in April. The nurse called Billy and Stephanie and told them, they could come and pick up their Easter Bunny. What a blessed, happy Easter for all.

Ernie Young, my 2nd husband officiated at the wedding. Billy and Stephanie got married in the fall and soon after, Billy was transferred with his job to Goshen, Indiana. Early the next year they moved back to the Lancaster area. I was happy that I would get to see my little grand baby more often.

Billy and Stephanie had three beautiful daughters, Shanelle, Ashley and Alyssa. I am so proud of them they are everything a grandparent would hope for.

Ernie, Actor and Priest

I met Ernie in the eighties. I had been cast in a play with a new dinner theatre in Lancaster called Rainbow Dinner Theatre. The owners and director of the theatre were looking for an actor to play my husband in the play, *"Any Wednesday."* The evening Ernie arrived from New York City, we actors in the play, were waiting for him, so we could do what you call a "read through" of the script. When he walked into the room, I looked at him and couldn't believe my eyes. Ernie was tall, handsome and had the most magnificent deep speaking voice. At that moment a thought ran through my mind, *one day you're going to marry him*. I thought it was awful for me to think such a thing, how could I, I was married. I guess you can't help the thoughts in your mind. I'm just trying to be honest.

Ernie and I were performing a play for Rainbow Dinner Theatre, when I received the news of Bill's death. I was in shock! I was concerned about how I was going to have a funeral without missing the show that I was in, since I didn't have an understudy. I planned the funeral so I would not miss work. The viewing was on Sunday and the funeral was Monday. I went back to work the next day and wondered how

I was going to get through the show without falling apart. The actors wanted to talk to me before the start of the show, but I told them not to speak to me until after the show was over. This was the only way I could get though the next two hours without breaking down. I almost fainted on stage that day and Cindy noticed there was something wrong with me, so she had the smelling salts waiting for me when I walked off stage. Life must go on.

Chris and Billy, now had another lifetime event to conquer, with the death of their father. Sometimes children must grow up faster then they should. I don't know of any child who has been through the trauma that my children have been through.

About a month after Ernie and I met he told me he was also an Episcopal priest. I was so shocked! An actor and a priest, this was hard for me to believe, but it was true. His given name was, Ernest Samuel Young. He attended Lehigh in Bethlehem with a full scholarship in English, and on to the Theological Seminary in Virginia. His first full time church was, Mt. Pocono, Pa. He was married with one son. When his marriage didn't last, Ernie was transferred to a church in New Jersey.

When I meant Ernie, he was semi retired from the church as a full time priest, and only filled in for priests who were away or on vacation. This gave him time to do voice overs, commercials for television and acting. I met Ernie in the 1980's a few years before Bill died. Both men liked each other and the one thing they both had in common, was smoking. I hated smoking and said I would never marry another man who smoked. So much for that!

Ernie proposed four years after Bill died and I said yes. When he asked me to marry him, he said, "Marry me and you'll always be young." I knew we would have a wonderful life together. I was very happy married to Ernie, he was a good listener and so tender when he spoke. He would be reading and I would just start talking, and he would always put his paper or book down, smile look up at me and say, "What dear, or sweetheart?" "Darling" was also a favorite name for me. We kissed, and told each other several times a day, "I love you." It was so wonderful being married to a man who was so affectionate and loving.

The day we got married is so clear in my mind. I was a happy 51 year old grandmother. Our wedding ceremony was held at the oldest inland Episcopal Church in the United States, Churchtown, Pa. June 7, 1991. The Bangor church was over flowing. It was a glorious perfect day. What fun, with my four year old grandchild Shanelle, as my flower girl and her reaction to riding in the limo from the church to our wedding reception was priceless. Shanelle said, "Look Grammy, we have a television and soda in the car." She was very impressed! I had planned on a small wedding, but my friends said they just had to attend, so it grew into at least 200 people. The church only held 200 people and some had to stand in the back of the church. What a beautiful, perfect day!

The day after the wedding we were in a limo, on our way to our cruise ship in New York City, the Queen Elizabeth ll for a transatlantic cruise to England. From the ship, a taxi picked us up and we headed to London for a one night stay. The next morning we were on our tour bus for a 10 day tour though England and Scotland. What a fantastic honeymoon! After our flight home, it all seemed like a dream. I wondered, how it could it be possible that I had visited so many wonderful places. I have such fond memories, and as they say, they will last a lifetime. We continued to make wonderful memories for 6 years. The years flew by so quickly. We loved to travel and traveled whenever we could.

Grandpa Ernie loved our little granddaughters and they loved to have him read to them. They would climb up in his lap and he would read story after story to them. Ernie had a great voice for story telling.

Billy and Ashley almost 2 yr.

Grammy Dollie and Shanelle 3 yr.

My sister Billie and me.

The Wreck

A few years after Ernie and I were married we moved to Leola. It was the perfect ranch style house for us and close to shopping. Little did I know just how perfect the Leola house was, until May 1997. This was the date my life changed again, and the world as I know it, almost ended.

Ernie was a history buff and wanted to follow the Cumberland Trail though some of the Southern states by car. It was so much fun just taking our time and stopping to see the historical sights. We started out on our quest the middle of May and planned to be home in a week.

It was May 23, 1997, a beautiful morning, Friday, about 9am, the first day of Memorial weekend. The sun was shining, the roads were clear and not much traffic. Ernie had been driving for the past six days, so I decided to drive for a few hours. We were driving a Lincoln, a big heavy car, I adjusted my seat and rear view mirror and fastened my seat belt. I had only been driving a short time when the wreck happened. We were hit head on by a SUV heading in the opposite direction on interstate 79 in West Virginia. We were about 40 miles from Morgantown.

I had set my cruise speed just under 65 miles per hour and I thought we'd have a relaxing drive for the next few hours. It's very difficult for me to describe what happened next. I have tried to remember, but I can only recall bits and pieces of the accident. I saw something flying through the sky, coming directly at me. This was the suburban heading right into my window, head on, like a big flash of light. From then on, everything is just a big blur and I think that's a good thing. My mind and body didn't want me to remember what happened or the terrible pain I was going through. Just like a women giving birth to a child, when it's all over you don't remember the awful pain.

A young man, Johnny Brown, was one of the first on the scene of the crash. Days later when he came to see me, at the hospital, Johnny told me he heard the crash while working at his business and knew what had happened, so he headed right for the wreck. He had a towing service not far from the crash sight.

This is the story he told me. First he checked me and after assessing my injuries, he knew there was nothing he could do for me. The top of the car had been crashed on top of me and the car engine had come back and crushed my legs. He then went to Ernie's side of the car, opened the door, unfastened his seatbelt, and asked him if he hurt anywhere. Ernie said, "My wrist." John pulled him out of the car and leaned him up on a nearby bank and went back to see if there was anything he could do for me.

The State Police and emergency crew arrived . The SUV had a family of five, parents and three children inside. Two of the children had broken bones and the other three had cuts and were banged up a bit. They were all taken to the hospital in Morgantown along with Ernie.

In the mean-time, the fire department was trying to cut me from the car. First the top of the car had to be cut off and that's when they discovered they couldn't move me, because the emergency break was imbedded in the back of my left thigh. The medics thought it was pressing on an artery, so they were afraid to move me for fear, I would bleed out.

Johnny Brown, the man I consider my angel, saved my life that day. He said I had been trapped over two hours and someone had to make a decision, or I would have no chance of survival. He took the jaws of life, and got under me and cut the break off where it entered my leg. Then I was transported to the hospital by helicopter.

I don't remember anything until four days later. It took 12 hours of surgery for the surgeons to rebuild my legs. My left femur was broken in 3 pieces, and I had very deep cuts, a broken ankle and deep nerve damage. The right leg was severely damaged, from the knee down to the ankle all the bones were crushed, along with deep cuts. My doctor said, "Your ankle looks like a crushed egg shell." The doctors attached what is called an external fixator on my leg and this was holding my bones and ankle together with wires, nails, skews, and plates. Also, all of my ribs were broken. Later I was told, I was lucky the doctors could save my right leg.

Life support kept me alive for the next three days. Then I was moved to a step down unit and had problems with my heart, so I was moved back to ICU. I'm not sure, but it was the fourth or fifth day, when I was moved to a private room. As I was being placed into the bed, I heard a voice yell, "Don't drop her leg, be more carful with my aunt!" This is when I started to become aware of my surroundings. The voice I heard was my niece, Kathy.

I then realized that I had been in a car wreck. The first words out of my mouth was, "Where is Ernie and what happened?" My son Bill, his wife, my sister Billie, nieces Kathy and Laurie, Ernie's sister and other relatives were all at the hospital. I had so much love and support around me and my heart was filled with love for all my family members.

Once I was fully aware of my surroundings, I had so many questions. I was confused and needed answers! Why am I still here? Why wasn't I killed? Most people with my injuries wouldn't have survived, so why am I still alive? I ask God this question over and over again. Finally, I knew the answer. My work here on earth wasn't finished, there was still something I was supposed to do. But what was it? It would take me months to figure this question out.

I asked about Ernie and they told me he was on life support. I thought, "Oh good he's alive!" The doctors said he was "brain dead." I was in shock and now trying to figure out what had happened to us. I looked down and saw that I had a cast, on the left leg and on the right leg, there were wires, rods and something that looked like a horseshoe and it was holding all the extra steel and rods together. I had screws in both ankles, a 9 inch steel plate in my lower right leg with screws holding the plate in place. The pain was terrible when I tried to move. My broken ribs were giving me a lot of pain whenever I tried to move, but in time they would heal.

The doctors kept me very sedated, but I could still think and ask questions. Later in the day the emergency room doctor, who was in charge of the ER when Ernie was admitted to the hospital, came to my room to tell me what had happened.

He sat in a chair across from me, and this is what he told me. "When your husband arrived at the hospital, we put him in a room and told him that we would get back to him. There were injured children brought into the ER and we needed to treat them. The children had some broken bones, so we attended to them and finally got back to your husband, when we discovered his heart had stopped beating. I manually opened his chest and massaged his heart for 15 minutes without success. I had stopped and was ready to call the time of death, when his heart started to beat again, so I put him on life support." The doctor then told me that Ernie was brain dead and they wanted me to give them permission to take him off life support.

I was alone in my room when this information was given to me. I was stunned! I couldn't believe what I had been told. My husband is brain dead! I didn't believe this and wanted to go see him. He was on another floor, so my bed was wheeled out to the elevator and to Ernie's room. I could see him hooked up to all kinds of equipment and thought this must have been what I looked like on life support. His head had a few pillows behind him and his eyes were open a little. I thought he was awake, but was told that was normal. After about 20 minutes, I was told I must go back to my room.

I went to see Ernie every day. The hospital kept pressuring me to take him off life support, but I wouldn't. I had a few more tests run on his brain to make sure his brain was dead. I told the doctor, when I was well enough to be airlifted back to a local hospital, where I lived, then I would consider taking my husband off life support. I thought, both of us would go home at the same time. I had to get my mind around the fact, that I was going to lose husband number two. How could this happen to me?

A few days after I had been moved to a private room, and I received a visitor, Johnny Brown. He stood in my door way and told me who he was and ask me if I remembered him. I did not remember him. Johnny said he had to come to the hospital to tell me that he didn't leave me. He said I was pleading with him, not to leave me or I would die. Johnny had been calling the hospital every day to check on my condition. When I could have visitors , he wanted to tell me, "I never left you." He said it was very important that he tell me this in person. He looked like an angel standing in my doorway with the sunlight shinning in on him. He never came any closer than the doorway and he looked like he had a halo shining over his head. To this day he will always be, my angel. It's because of Johnny that I am alive today.

My son was working with my family doctor to arrange my transfer to Lancaster General Hospital. The hospital told me, I was too ill to be transferred, but I was determined to go home. Billy had taken time from his business to stay with me at the hospital. My family doctor and son arranged to have an air ambulance transport me to Lancaster. I remember the male nurse who took care of me on the flight. He was a big, burly man, and I told him that I was afraid I would roll off the bed in the plane, with the plane moving and turning on takeoff. He told me not to worry, he had been a medic in the Vietnam war, and he wouldn't let anything happen to me. He would make sure I was safe. The medic sat on the floor of the plane, and leaned his back up against my bed, so I would feel safe and wouldn't roll off. I was afraid of hitting my legs, with all the hardware plus the cast. He was so kind and told me interesting stories to make the time in the plane pass more quickly.

Ernie's birthday was May 26, while on life support. He turned 60 years young. I recall during our marriage, when we were traveling by car and came upon an accident with injuries, he would always park the car and walk over the the accident to see if he could be of any emotional help to the injured. The day before I was to be flown to Lancaster, the hospital took Ernie off life support.

We both had "living wills" and were organ donors. Because his heart had stopped for such a long time the only part of his body that could be used for transplant was his beautiful blue eyes. I am filled with joy, to know that someone can see again, due to the gift of Ernie's eyes. Sometimes I wonder who received his eyes. This makes me very happy.

There was an Episcopal Church in Morgantown, and I knew the Rector of the church would want to be informed about Ernie's medical condition, since Ernie was also an Episcopal Priest. The priest came to the hospital every day to pray for Ernie. He was so devoted, I couldn't believe that he was there every day! A year later I went back to the church to present them, with a donation in memory of "Father Ernest S.Young".

I was in Ernie's room when he was taken off life support. The doctor prepared me by saying, "He may breathe on his own for a few minutes." About 20 minutes had gone by and he was still breathing on his own. This seemed to give me some hope and I was told again, that sometimes this happens. I was taken back to my room and Billy said he would stay with Ernie. Billy said, " About an hour had gone by, I took hold of Ernie's shoulders, shook him and said, you can go now, and he took a deep breath, let it out, and it was all over, he was gone." It was as if he was asking permission to go, to leave this earth, to go home to God.

It took about 3 hours from the time I left Morgantown and was settled in my new room at Lancaster General Hospital. As I lay in my bed I thought about everything that had taken place in the past few weeks. It was all a big blur to me, it was like I was in a daze. I wanted to wake up from a bad dream. How could this have happened to me? The next day, it really hit me! I thought……oh dear God, now I have to plan a funeral for my husband and I'm a patient in the hospital. How was I going to do this? I'm being honest when I say, I don't remember all the details.

News about our accident had made the TV news and the local newspapers. The news was such a shock to friends and local people. They all showed their love and concern in so many ways. I had so many flowers in my hospital room that there weren't enough places to put them, so some had to be set outside my room on tables. Cards and flowers do so much for a person who is ill or in the hospital. One woman I worked with sent me a card every week for a year, even when she was on vacation. I will never forget her kindness and compassion.

Tom Stradling came to the hospital to see if he could help me in any way with Ernie's funeral. The Stradling Funeral Homes, founded by George and Jane, had been in charge of Mark and Bill's funerals. When Tom came to my hospital room we talked and I said I don't know how I'm going to do this. Tom said, that he would take care of the arrangements for me and not to worry. I was so relieved and I knew I could trust him to make the right choices for me. He did, right down to the most beautiful flowers draping the casket that I had ever seen.

Now I had another problem. How was I going to get from the hospital to my husband's funeral? I asked the social worker at LGH to come to my room and I told her, "I don't know how you're going to accomplish this, but I'm going! I will leave it up to you to figure out a way to get me there." She said, " they would work it out somehow," and they did.

The day of the funeral my IV line was removed for the trip from Lancaster to Akron. The hospital had a new van for patients in a wheel chair and it was used to transport me. My son and his wife rode along with me. There were pillows under my legs and covered with a blanket. I thought it would be better if friends couldn't see how bad my legs looked. The ride was very painful and every little bump was felt by my legs. Billy held my legs trying to reduce my pain and I could see his eyes tearing.

The funeral home was filled with relatives and friends by the time I arrived. I prayed to God, to please help me get through this without breaking down. God answered my prayer. I looked around and saw my sweet little granddaughters. This was the first funeral for them and I wondered what they were thinking. One of them said, "Grandpa looks like he's wearing a Halloween mask." From a child's viewpoint, I thought that was a very interesting observation.

The priest who officiated for the service was so wonderful. He had never met my husband, but captured him perfectly, by speaking to the guests before the funeral started. At one point during the service, the guests were ask by the clergy to give Ernie, "the applause he so richly deserved." Everyone stood up and gave him a standing ovation. The applause continued for sometime. Ernie would have been so thrilled and honored. My emotions were running away with me and I was so proud. I'm sure Ernie was there looking down on the guests.

The day of Ernie's funeral, we had been married six years. Over the years, we discussed what each other's wishes would be when we passed on, and he always said, "Just put me in a pine box, like the Amish, I don't need anything fancy." I told him I'd never do that, but he had one request, bag pipes playing "Amazing Grace." His request was honored. My friends carried my wheelchair, with me sitting in it, from the van to the grave site. The ground was too rough to push the chair. It was all over so quickly and before I knew it, I was back in my hospital bed. I was exhausted!

Most days I would have therapy twice a day in the morning and afternoon, for a total of 3 hours. The object of my therapy was to transfer myself from my bed, onto a transfer board, by putting the board underneath me, and use my arms and hands to lift my body onto the board and use my hands to transfer to a wheel chair or a potty chair. My ribs had not healed and this caused so much pain. The hospital ask for a family member to be with me the first day of therapy, and Billy volunteered. My nurse gave me double pain pills before my therapy and when I asked why, she said, " You'll need them." Boy, was she right!

When Billy saw how much difficulty I was having trying to lift my body onto a transfer board, he jumped up to help me, and was told, he couldn't help, I had to learn to do it myself. Later he told me, that was the hardest thing he ever had to do, watching me, and seeing how much pain I was in. That night I was so tired and weak from the funeral that I couldn't transfer myself. I pressed my call button for the nurse, she came to the room, because I was not to try this without having a nurse with me. I started to cry because my arms were so weak, I couldn't transfer myself and my nurse said she would call for help. A very large man entered my room, he lifted me from my bed and placed me on the potty chair. He was a very kind man, and a male nurse. The nurse left my room and returned a few minutes later. He stayed for a few minutes and when he told me he was a single father, I thought his child was so lucky to have such a caring parent.

A requirement to leave the hospital was to transfer myself, with no help from anyone. I worked very hard, because the only thing I wanted was to go home, and this was the only way it would ever happen. It would be months before I could walk and take care of myself.

Before I went home, I had to have a wheelchair ramp built. Rick, a wonderful friend, gave up his vacation to build the ramp for me. And I will always be so grateful to him. A hospital bed had to be set up in my family room. There was no way I could climb in and out of my own bed. I was so glad my house was a ranch style, this would make it possible in the weeks ahead, to maneuver around the house in a wheelchair.

I slept on my back for about 3 months, with all the hardware on my right leg, I couldn't sleep any other way. The back of my heels got so sore from touching the bed sheets, and putting cream on them didn't help much, so I would let my feet hang over the end of the bed. I so desperately wanted to sleep on my side, and longed for that day to come. A wheelchair van drove me to my doctor's appointments, and I had 24 hour care at home. A therapist came to the house 3 times a week. I saw him more than my family, and he became like a member of my family.

My main nurse was also like a member of my family. She cared for me at the house at least 5 days a week. Peggy was a wonderful caring, loving and thoughtful person. My family doctor's office was only about 2 blocks away, so when I had an appointment with Dr. Samitt, she would push me to his office in my wheelchair. Peggy didn't like just sitting around waiting for me to need her, so she would do little jobs in my house to keep herself busy. She was one of a kind.

One day I ask Peggy if she would drive me to Landis Homes, where I worked as an insurance counselor. Over the months I had received so many cards, letters and words of encouragement from my dear friends at Landis Homes, they were like family to me. I loved them and missed seeing them. Seniors today have been through so much in their lifetime, and know how to show they care, with love and compassion.

I'll never forget the day when the Chaplain, Don Good, from Landis Homes called me and ask if he could come to the house for a visit. He sounded very mysterious on the phone, and I wondered what it could be. We visited a few minutes and he pulled an envelope out of his coat and gave it to me. When I opened it, there was a check for several hundred dollars. When church was held on the previous Sunday, the members came to him and said, "We'd like our collection today to go to Dollie." He then told me, " This should show you how much the residents at Landis Homes think of you. This is the first time they have ever given a collection to an individual . They usually give it to a mission fund or something to do with the church." I couldn't believe what had just happened. I didn't want to take the check, but he said they really wanted me to have it. I was so honored, what great people, and not because they gave me a check, but because, they are special, they are real, loving and generous people. I loved them all and I'm sure there is a special place in Heaven for them. I was looking forward to the day when I would be able to resume my duties as Insurance Counselor at Landis Homes.

One day Jane and Kay, two of my friends, came to my house to play bridge, a card game. You need four people to play, but we only had three, so we dealt four hands and the high bidder got the fourth hand. I was still confined to my bed, so we put a tray on my lap, Jane sat in the wheelchair and Kay sat on my potty chair. We had a ball that day. It was so much fun and we had a few good laughs too. Remember, laughter is good for the soul, it helps you live longer and look younger.

I was becoming more restless with each passing day. How much television can a person watch? How can there be so many channels to choose from and still nothing to watch? I was so bored! I bought a computer from a home shopping channel and I didn't know the first thing about a personal computer, but I thought this was a good time to learn. Shanelle, my granddaughter who was only 10 years old said, " Grammy, do you want me to setup the computer for you?" I couldn't believe someone so young had so much knowledge. She knew exactly what she was doing.

About three months had passed and I had surgery to remove the hardware from my right leg. I was thrilled to have this contraption removed, finally I could walk with a walker and take a shower. I had to wear a boot on my leg during the day. It felt like forever since I had slept on my side, since I had to be flat on my back until the hardware was removed. And most of all, to finally sleep in my own bed. The little things are so important.

My dad's four sisters, from Ohio, surprised me with a visit. They told me that since my dad wasn't alive, that they would take his place and come and visit me. What a happy occasion this was. I couldn't believe they were doing this for me. My four aunts, Ruth, Ethel, Judy and Doris, had never been on a trip together before. This was a first for them and very special. They stayed one day and night before they started back home. I'll always be so grateful for the effort they made for me and my dad. Other visitors I had in those early weeks, were my Aunt Edith, my mom's youngest sister from Denver. She stayed two weeks and my sister Erlene, from Iowa came for a week. The next month, my niece Kathy joined me for a week. She cleaned house and organized my basement. Kathy doesn't waste anytime getting things done, she's a real go-getter! It was such a wonderful treat to have Kathy spend the week with me, and the time passed all too quickly.

Doctor Samitt, my family doctor, wanted to see me every two weeks, to follow my care. He and his office staff became very good friends with me. A nurse came to the house everyday to give me a shot in the stomach, it was a blood thinner. Since I wasn't active and had so much hardware on and in my legs, I needed the shot to decrease the chance of getting a blood clot.

I can't say enough kind words about Doctor Joel Samitt. What a dedicated doctor he was, kind, compassionate, thoughtful and caring. A few years ago, he retired and moved to Florida. I miss him a lot. There was a retirement party for him and his wife at his office, and when I arrived there was a long line outside the building. I wasn't surprised to see so many people. He told me he had no idea so many of his patients would come to his retirement party. He was so happy that day and I was happy for him. He was the most wonderful doctor I've ever had the pleasure to meet. I made sure I had an appointment with Dr. Samitt his last day, before he retired. I must admit, I cried and I saw a few tears in his eyes too. I will always be so grateful to him. One of a kind! My warm memories of Dr. Samitt will always be with me.

I had a bone graft in my right femur and tibia because the bones weren't healing. Bone was taken from my hip and packed in my leg, where the bones were crushed. After the surgery, as I was coming out of the anesthesia, I heard myself screaming. The nurse asked what was wrong, and I said, "I can't stand the pain. My leg feels like it is on fire!" The doctor came to check on me and my pain meds were increased to the maximum level. A few days later I was back home.

The day finally came, when I started to walk with a walker. It was like getting a Christmas gift. I could finally start doing some things for myself. Months later many of my friends told me, they thought I'd never walk again, and if I did walk, I would have a limp. I had faith and I knew that I would walk!

Seven months after the wreck, my orthopedic surgeon in Lancaster, thought my femur was healed, and removed the rod and screws that was holding my leg together. This surgery was the last week in December 1997. I stayed overnight in the hospital. It was a hospital rule after surgery, a patient had to go to therapy before they could be discharged. The moment I tried to stand for the first time after the surgery, I was filled with excruciating pain in my leg. I couldn't stand up and had to hang on to the bed so I wouldn't fall. The nurse said, " You'll have pain." I knew it shouldn't be the kind of pain I was experiencing. The therapist could see the agony I was in, and she had tears running down her face, and helped me get back in the wheelchair. I wondered, how many kinds of painful torture a person can take.

I won't go into a long story about what happened, but my son had to arrange for another hospital bed at home. The pain was so bad I couldn't get in and out of my bed, and again, I had to have a nurse everyday. I called the doctors office many times in the next ten days. They didn't want to see me unless I had a fever. A few times my pain medication was changed, but it never helped me. I was in so much pain it took me at least 20 minutes to move from my bed to wheelchair, an inch at a time. Everything was in slow motion and trying not to move my leg. I knew there was something wrong with my femur, but the doctors wouldn't listen to me. A patient knows their body better than the doctor!

My friend Liz had come for a visit, took one look at me and said, "You should get to a doctor!" I knew the doctor wouldn't see me, because I didn't have a fever, so I told them my thermometer was broken, and the office said, for me to come in right away. Liz knew what I was going through. She had fallen from a ladder about a year earlier, when she was trying to cut a tree branch and did a lot of damage to her leg. Liz drove me to the doctors in my car, because it had leather seats and I could sit on the edge of the seat and slide my body on the leather without moving my leg a lot. This helped with the pain.

The doctor saw how difficult it was for me to move, so he went to x-ray with me and held me up during the x-rays. There was no way they could get me on a table with the pain I was in. I wasn't surprised when I was told my femur was broken. I knew it all along! The rod was removed before the bone had healed. When they x-rayed after surgery, in the operating room, the leg looked healed, but it wasn't. The first time I stood, the broken bones separated again.

My doctor phoned the ambulance to transport me to the trauma center. Before I knew it, there were two police officers in my room. Why were they here? I was told, when an ambulance is call for transport, that the police also arrive on the scene. This time I had to be at a trauma center, because of the type injury I had. My leg needed a rod placed in the femur again. I was on an antibiotic for 48 hours before the surgery, to protect me from infection, because of cutting into the deepest part of my body again. I know my doctor was worried about me, because the next morning very early, he was in my room checking on me and it was on a Sunday. From May 1997 to January 1998, I had surgery seven times; I still have the rod in my leg today. In both legs, I have 19 pieces of hardware. I prayed that I would not need anymore surgery on my legs and that prayer has come true.

Every night before I would to to bed, I made list of the things in my life that I was thankful for. I would say a prayer to God, and after that, I would lie in bed and say the "Lord's Prayer" over and over again until I fell to sleep. I found so many meanings in the words, just saying them slowly and thinking about each word. Try it sometime!

Being home bound is no fun, I was going crazy and just had to get out of the house. First I needed a car, and thought, if I got a car I could talk the doctor into letting me drive. My son said ,"Mom, if you call the car dealer, they'll bring a car out for you to see and drive." I thought this was a great idea. Sure enough, I told them what I wanted and later in the day there was a young man at my door with a very nice car for me to see. When I opened the door, standing in front of him with a walker, I figured he'd leave. I said, "Are you afraid to ride with me in a car?" And he said,"No, I'm a Marine!," I bought the car that day.

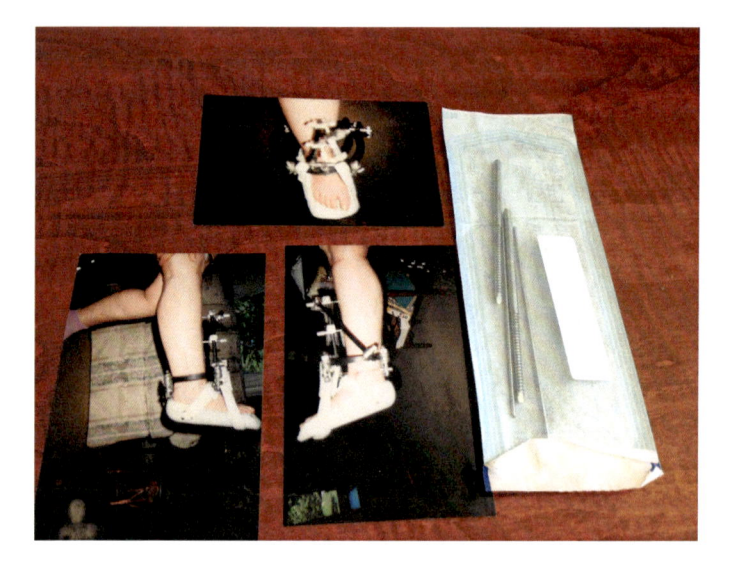

This is a picture of some of the hardware that I wore on my leg for 3 months.

God's Plan

It was now a new year, with new adventures in my life ,and I wondered what was ahead for me. I wanted to write a book about my life, but one thing always on my mind, was more information about the car wreck. Billy, drove me back to Morgantown to interview the state trooper who was at the scene of the accident. I ask him why he never finished an accident report on me and he told me, "Because I didn't think you were going to survive the wreck." I didn't know what to say, I was in shock! The trooper didn't want to do the accident report over, if I died, so he just didn't finish it. When I got home I thought about this a lot and wondered, why am I still alive? What's the answer to this question? I knew God wanted me to live, but why? I ask myself the same question over and over again.

One morning I woke up and my face was wet with tears. I had been dreaming. During my dream, I saw Ernie standing at the end of my bed, and I was telling him, "I want to go with you." He said, "No, you can't! Your work here isn't finished." My dream was so real and I wondered what it meant, what was I supposed to do with my life? This question was on my mind for many months.

I knew God had plans for me and I had to figure out what He wanted me to do, with the rest of my life. There was a reason I didn't die in the car accident. What was it? It would take me a few years to figure this out.

About three years later, my son asked me if I wanted to buy the old church building from the fire department in Christiana. They had used the building for supplies and storage for the smaller trucks. The fire department had given him first choice on the building, because he had helped them so much, by letting them use his large parking lot when they had auctions to raise funds for the fire company.

One day, when I was driving though the farmland, it came to me.......I was to buy an old church building in Christiana, PA. It was built around 1857, but what was I to do with this building? Should I to start a new church? After all my grandfather and four of my cousins are ministers. Finally the day came and I knew what I was to do with the building. Turn it into a small unique dinner theatre. I did have some doubts, but I followed the little voice inside me. We spent 19 months gutting and restoring the old church to turn it into a dinner theatre.

Experience, with dinner theatre and community theatre, was something I had knowledge about. Being involved with the Ephrata Performing Arts Center for years and on stage with

Rainbow Dinner Theatre and becoming their director of marketing, I felt I should give it a try. There were so many questions. What kinds of shows should I do? There were already two dinner theatres in in my area; one did musicals and the other comedy. My shows should be different, but how? We would have plenty of time to make this decision in the months ahead.

Dollie and Lionel in 2001 the year we were married.

Third Time's Charm

I met Lionel Caldwell in January 2000 and we started dating. I told myself I was never getting married again after being widowed two times, and I honestly believed this. Lionel had gone through a divorce after many years of marriage and two children. We were matched up on a blind date by a friend. I wondered if I should meet someone else, because I had had a few dates and they were all very nice men, but no one I could see a future with, so I finally decided to meet Lionel. We had such a good time talking ,and he seemed so sweet, so we exchanged phone numbers. I went home thinking I would never see him or hear from him again. A few days later I was in the Akron Restaurant with my friend Lynn. We had met for breakfast so I could tell her about my blind date. As I was giving her the details of my date with Lionel, guess who walked into the restaurant? Yes, it was Lionel. We were both in shock when we saw each other. What are the odds of this "chance meeting?" I looked at this as a sign and decided if he ever called me, I would see him again. Lionel called me soon after our first meeting and we started dating.

My friend Carole and I decided to go on a cruise, and when Lionel found out, he said, "Can I go with you?" Of course I had to tell him no, and when I walked into my cabin on the ship, there was a beautiful arrangement of flowers, with a card from Lionel, telling me to have a wonderful cruise. I thought this was such a kind gesture and I knew he wanted me to remember him while on the cruise. When I returned home, he sent me beautiful emails and I thought, what a romantic writer. Well, I saved them all and he was surprised when I told him. Lionel told me he didn't remember what he wrote in the letters, so I told him that some day I would give them to him to read and we'd both have a good laugh.

We dated each other for over a year. When he ask me to marry him, I said, "Aren't you afraid to marry me, I've been widowed twice?" He said, "No, third time was the charm." We married on April 7, 2001. The wedding was held at our new home. Lionel and Dave, a friend, built a huge deck across the back of our house for the wedding. The guest sat in chairs on the lawn. My bridesmaids were Lionel's daughters, Casey, Maria and my granddaughters, Shanelle, Ashley, Alyssa and Sabrina. My son gave me away, and he and his wife also prepared fantastic food for the wedding. My good friend Jackie Rupp, provided beautiful music on the piano and the Reverend Alan Ruby conducted the wedding ceremony. There was music with dancing in the dining room, provided by Don and Liz Trostle. The wedding was attended by family and close friends. It was a perfect day.

A few days later we went on a cruise for our honeymoon. There's nothing better than a cruise to relax, with good food, sunshine and sunny romantic destinations. Our new life was beginning.

Billy age 4 and below his daughters. Ashley, Alyssa and Shanelle.

Freedom Chapel Dinner Theatre

Now it was time for a new chapter in my life to begin. The honeymoon was over and it was time to get back to business. The old church building over the years had been used as an antique shop, scout hall, and also, the Christiana Fire Department. It was about to be transformed into a charming, unique, dinner theatre. When I bought the building, the local Christiana Fire Department kept their supplies and smaller trucks inside.

First I had to surround myself with experts in their fields, so that they could transform my 1850's building into the magical place, I knew it could become. Tibbits and Weaver in Lancaster were the architects, and Victor Capecce was the designer. Victor had such a fabulous vision, and the design he drew was breath taking. I now knew what my theater would look like when it was finished. My husband Lionel, was the General Contractor and many others, too numerous to mention, gave of their time and skills to make my dream come true. Every person who worked on our project went the extra mile for us.

Nineteen months is a long time to prepare a building for its grand opening. We worked very long hours around the clock during this time. Freedom Chapel's doors opened in April, 2003. I was so happy and proud. All members of the Lancaster County Visitors Bureau were invited to attend our open house and we had standing room only. What an exciting evening, with great food and conversation. All of our hard work had paid off!

Now it was time to open our World Premier, and my first play as a playwright with "The Treason Trials of 1851." This was the perfect opening for Freedom Chapel Dinner Theatre. The play is about slavery and what led to the largest "treason trial" in our nations history. Thirty-eight men were arrested for treason and levying war against the United States Government, because they wouldn't help a US Marshall capture runaway slaves at the William Parker home. Parker was also a runaway slave, but people living in the area thought he was a free man. He had run away years earlier from a slave owner in Maryland. The trial took place in Independence Hall in Philadelphia, where our nation was founded, ten years before the Civil War. If you're interested in reading more about this incident which took place on 9/11/1851, research William Parker, The Freeman Story and the Christiana Riot. This is a fascinating true story, about slavery and the Underground Railroad. Many buildings and homes in Christiana had hiding places and were used as stations on the Underground Railroad.

Oh, I guess I should tell you, the theatre was also haunted. Many strange incidents happened over the years. One day I was working at my computer, and I saw someone walk by the french doors on the balcony. I opened the door and looked out on the balcony and the adjoining rooms and didn't see anyone. The office staff laughted, but I knew what I saw! The lights in the building would all be turned off when we went home for the day and the next morning when we arrived, they would be turned on. Our stage lighting panel, with controls, would be moved around and not where we left them at the end of the day. Our ghosts were friendly and would show up in pictures in the form of orbs. I have friends who came to me and said, "We know you have ghosts. We can feel their presence in the building." The ghosts or spirits, whatever you choose to call them, always made an appearance when a wedding took place in the theatre. This presence was very strong, near the front of the building. Once the original floor was exposed, we found a trap door with steps leading to the basement. In the basement there was a stone wall with a doorway into a small room with all stone walls. The architect for the theatre, said the room in the basement had to be there for a reason, and thought it may have been used to hide slaves. It was very unusual to have a room like this in a church basement. The little town of Christiana, was very important in the Underground Railroad movement, before and during the Civil War. Many Quakers, who settled this area, came to the aid of runaway slaves, searching for their freedom. A great number of the runaway slaves fled to

Canada and settled in Ontario. Once in Canada, the slaves would be free and could even own property.

The Amish shows were true, based on real life of the local Amish. I had been a tour guide for many years, and some of the questions tourists ask me concerning the Amish, you would not believe. For example, "Are they Americans, or What do they use for money?" So, I thought it was about time I address some of their unbelievable questions, by writing true stories about the customs of the Amish. The tourists always wanted to know about weddings, Christmas and holidays, church, funerals, cars, horses and buggies and the list goes on and on. What better way to answer their questions, than to see live actors portraying Amish and dressed as Amish.

Even the local Amish came to see my Amish shows. A few of them saw many of my shows and would bring other family members back with them. An Amish lady brought her mother for her 80th birthday. An Amish Minster, whose wife had been to see the show with a group of other Amish women, brought her husband. After the show, I smiled at him and he said, "I guess I had to come and see the show to see how I really am." We both laughed with approval.

After a shooting at a local Amish school, we wanted to show our support, so we performed a benefit show for the Nickel Mines Amish School, with all the proceeds going to the families of the children. After the benefit, I wanted to speak to one of the families who had lost two children, since I had also lost two children. Arrangements were made for me to visit them after the terrible tragedy. I told the Amish mother, that I had also lost two children, and she wanted to know all the details. We bonded that day and she ended up consoling me as I felt the tears falling down my face for the loss that we both shared. This was indeed a special moment for us both. We both shared a tragic event and planned to meet again in the future.

We continued to perform shows at Freedom Chapel Dinner Theatre through the end of December 2010. During the years we were open I wrote one historical play, "The Treason Trials of 1851" and five Amish shows, all based on true facts and stories. They are; *"Amish Vows in Paradise, Amish Family Christmas, Amish Love and Forgiveness, Amish Acres the Next Generation and Amish and Amish Reunion.* The play "Amish Vows in Paradise", also went on tour in Spain as a mission project for the Berks Christian School. The students did the play in english (as most people in Spain speak english) with sub-titles above. Spain loved the Amish show and said they would like to see more of them. I was very pleased to be welcomed by the Spanish population with great enthusiasm.

Bird-in-Hand Restaurant, also partnered with me and I did two seasons of Amish shows at their restaurant with an Amish style wedding meal. It seemed like people just couldn't get enough information about the Amish. There is so much information circulating around the country that is false and made up and I wanted to set the record straight. Over the years many Amish and local people came to see my shows and told me how proud they were, that I was so honest in portraying the Amish. I considered the local Amish my friends and wanted people to learn about their *true* beliefs, their Christian faith and how important family life was to my dear Amish Friends.

Artist sketch of Freedom Chapel Dinner Theatre
by Victor Capecce theatre designer.

The Canadian Connection

The day I met Bradley Walters changed my life. Little did I know that this would be the beginning of a wonderful friendship with the Walters Family. When I attended the Ontario Motorcoach Association to promote my dinner theatre to tour companies that were traveling to my area, was the day I met Bradley. Bradley was promoting his business Bradley Walters Journeys. When you travel with Bradley you can be assured that he has personally spent days, and weeks planning your getaway. His Journeys travel all over the world. When I told him I had a dinner theatre and we performed true Amish shows. He was very interested. Bradley gave me a brochure about his families dinner theatre and we bonded instantly.

Bradley ask me to call his brother Darren and inform him about my shows. I thought about making that call for months and the day I was reaching for the phone to call Darren Walters, my phone rang. It was Darren. He ask me about my shows and I sent him a script for "Amish Vows in Paradise". The following year we were at the Walters Dinner Theatre" in Bright, Ontario with the show. The actors who had made the show such a success in Lancaster County, traveled with me for our opening in Canada. How exciting for all of us. The Walters Theatre was beautiful. It was an old barn that had been converted into a beautiful dinner theatre. It even had a hanging chandelier in the ladies restroom.

The guest attending their shows would be seated at round tables for the meal and move to theatre seats in the center of the room for the show. The theatre was located in the county and as you arrived, there was a split rail fence lining the front of the 100 acre ranch, with a tall beautiful cast iron gate and glorious flowers planted everywhere you looked. You would then drive the long blacktop lane past beautiful pine trees and a welcoming pond with swans floating in it. Around the pond was outdoor furniture for relaxing before the show. Many guest arrived early just to enjoy the well manicured grounds. As you approached you also saw the family home centuries old built with beautiful stone, plus other buildings surrounding the property.

Decorating the wooden walls of the theatre you see poster after poster, of famous entertainers who are friends of the Walters Family. They also performed with many of them in their shows. The Walters Family are country entertainers, who have appeared on such prestigious stages as The Ryman Auditorium in Nashville. Darren, Bradley, Kimberly, Shirley and Gary, the mom and dad. On a sad note, Gary passed away a few years ago. Most recently joining the family group is young Schyler, son of Kim. Thousands of fans have enjoyed the fiddling, great singing and comedy of the talented Walters

Family for years, may it be Concert Halls, Cruise Ships or television. The family have recorded numerous CD's over the years featuring many types of music. The Walters Family, is one of the most talented and loving families you could ever meet. I love and respect them very much.

Over the past years I have performed all of my Amish shows on the Walters stage and some of them even twice. We also brought some well known shows to their stage such as, Driving Miss Daisy. A good friend, Jim Munro also wrote some wonderful comedy shows for me that graced the Walters stage. My shows were the first drama productions on their stage, I was very thrilled about the special honor being given to me. Most all of the shows on the Walters stage are musical performances

Darren told me that he'd like to be my manger and promote my shows in Canada. I was thrilled and so excited! Darren is such a considerate young man and worked very diligently for me, along side a promotor Brian Edwards. I can't thank them enough for all they've done for my Amish shows and making it possible for so many people across Canada to see them.

We thought we'd have a trial run and do a few shows in large theatres in the Ontario area, before we took the show on the road. The shows were very well received. So the next year, in November we went on our first "road tour."

What a fantastic tour! Lionel, my husband, the cast and of course myself, flew out of Harrisburg International Airport to

Winnipeg, Canada for a Western Canadian Tour with "Amish Family Christmas." We traveled from Winnipeg to Alberta and back performing the show at different theatre venues. We were very well received by the audiences in Canada, families, young folks and seniors. My heart was filled with joy and happiness for the welcome that was cast upon us during this special Christmas season.

I'll never forget one of our shows when near Alberta, during the show, we had a scene where we sing "Silent Night" in German. The audience of over 1000 joined in, singing in German, and it was beautiful. It sounded like the Morgan Tabernacle Choir, what a magical moment for all. It's a very joyful experience to bring the " true meaning of Christmas," as the Bible tells the story, to a grateful audience.

I'll never forget how nice the weather was on our more then two week tour. There was only a trace of snow, once. The weather was very dry and couldn't have been any better. Most of our traveling was through the prairie lands with a lot of crops and oil wells. I never saw so many oil wells in my life. Having the chance to visit towns like Red Deer, Moose Jaw and Medicine Hat was also very special. We all returned home a few days before Christmas with memories we will cherish forever.

The following year in November and December, we started our three week road tour in Ontario. We traveled over 5000 miles, up to Prince Edward Island, Nova Scotia, New Brunswick and Ottawa. This trip was just as wonderful as the previous year. Every where we traveled we met such appreciative people filled with gratitude and we were given such a wonderful reception.

Everyone was interested in the Amish, especially After the Nickel Mines Amish school shooting on October 2, 2006. The Amish made the national news. Man shoots 11 killing 5 girls in Amish School.

One evening we worried if we had enough gas to get us to the next destination. We had been driving for hours and it started to snow and was dark outside. There wasn't a gas station anywhere, so we turned around and went back, to where we saw a fuel station earlier. It's a good thing we did, because it was the only place we could get diesel fuel or we would have been stuck along the road side in a snow storm. Sometimes it all works out for the best!

Poutine, is a dish of French fries topped with cheese curds and gravy. One of the actors couldn't get enough of this Canadian dish. She ate it everyday for several days in a row. It is very good! Lobster, was in season, so we stopped and bought ten pounds. It was frozen cleaned and boneless, all ready to eat. The next day we ate lobster topped with butter in the breakfast room of our hotel, and it was enjoyed by all.

I was invited to be a guest on a radio show by the owner and manger after he saw," Amish Family Christmas." He told me his wife made him attend the show and he was so glad he did. He said," I never expected to see anything like what I saw tonight." The audience expressed their gratitude and appreciation with every performance. We always invited the guest up to the stage after the show, so we could answer any questions they had. After each show we would load the props into the van, arrive back at the hotel for a well deserved rest, and the next morning, head out for the next venue.

It was a dream of one of the actors to see "Ann of Green Gables" while we were on Prince Edward Island. We had some time for sight seeing the next morning, so six of us piled in the van on a quest for Ann of Green Gables. I guess we weren't very good at following directions, because we couldn't find it, and ended up driving around most of the island. After asking directions from a local, we finally arrived at our destination. And it was worth the trip!

During our drive around the island, we discovered some sand dunes. We stopped to take pictures and a few people decided to climb them. They wanted to see the view from the top. I stayed in the van and waited. When Lionel got back into the van, I noticed he had grass and straw on his jacket, and I missed the event of the day! Lionel had slipped and rolled all the way from the top to the bottom of the sand dune. I missed it, but someone snapped a picture of him rolling down. We all had a great time that day.

The comradely we all shared on the road trips, was very special. You become a family and form friendships that will last a lifetime. Darren Walters is a special jewel, and a very unique person. I will never forget all that he has done for me.

With his guidance and expertise both trips ran very smoothly. I will forever be grateful!

December 14, 2012 was the last day of our journey home. We were all happy and reminiscing about the past days of our road trip, when we came upon many state trooper cars along the side of the interstate in Connecticut. I turned on the car radio and we were in shock with the news, 20 children and 6 adults had been fatally shoot at a elementary school in Newtown, Connecticut. There was silence in the van, we were all in shock! We all called our homes after hearing this terrible news. How awful for the families and friends of the Newtown community. Very little was said during the finial hours of our trip home. We were all happy to arrive home safe and sound. In our thoughts we were thinking of the families who had just lost their loved ones.

Life does go on, it may seem like it stops, but it doesn't. No matter what you're personally going through in your life, the world still goes around. When tragic events take place in ones life, they will feel like they can't go on, and they just want to die. But you can go on, don't be a quitter, have faith in yourself, because you can do it. Remember to lean on your family and friends. And if you believe in God, He's there for you too. I know I wouldn't have gotten through all my life tragically's without having trust and belief in a higher power. I won't quit no matter what happens.

I'M NO QUITTER!

I'm No Quitter!

The Walters Family Dinner Theatre

The Walters Family

I'm No Quitter!

Rainbow Comedy Theatre in Paradise

EPAC The Ephrata Performing Arts Center

I'm No Quitter!

Erlene, Jerry, Dollie, and Billie

Maria, Lionel, and Casey